Communicating Across The Divides In Our Everyday Lives

A PSYCHOLOGICAL FIELD MANUAL

FOR CONSTRUCTIVE DIALOGUE

ABOUT SOCIAL AND ENVIRONMENTAL CONCERNS,

AND THE PROGRESS OF CIVILIZATION

DON SCHNEIDER

Elkdream Media

Over the course of more than thirty years of involvement
with the field of professional psychology, Dr. Schneider's focus has shifted
and broadened from the realm of our individual neuroses to the larger,
and arguably more urgent, social and environmental issues
facing us as a global community.

This book can be purchased online at lulu.com.
For bulk orders at a discounted price, contact Don at
communicating.across.the.divides@gmail.com
or elkdream_farm@yahoo.com or (541) 747-6677.
(permission to resell discounted bulk purchases at a profit
for yourself or your organization granted)

Communicating Across The Divides In Our Everyday Lives
December 2009 / Elkdream Media

Table of Contents

ACKNOWLEDGEMENTS

THERE HAVE BEEN TOO MANY WONDERFUL PEOPLE—teachers, colleagues, clients, authors, and friends—over the years to acknowledge them all. Forgiveness for any oversight is humbly requested along with sincere apologies for being unable to offer full proper recognition. Many have contributed in ways that they will never know. It is unlikely that I will ever be able to articulate clearly how their courage, generosity, and insights have become integrated into my own worldview and values. All have contributed to my growth and development as a human being, and to my current thinking (such as it is). For this I offer heartfelt appreciation.

For their steadfast love and support, as well as their tireless attempts to understand the complex person that I am and the unique path I have chosen, I want to offer a special thank you to my wife Elin, my children Kyra and Kory, my brother, father, sister, and mother. For their exemplary trail-blazing, inspiring leadership, and role modeling: Joanna and Fran Macy, and Dick and Jeanne Roy. For their multifarious contributions to my life: my many sustainability-oriented friends from the Pleasant Hill Progressives, the Eugene Permaculture Guild, Lost Valley Educational Center, Dharmalaya Center, Maitreya Ecovillage, my amazing Self-Organizing Men's Group, my wonderful local support groups and co-counselors, Tree Bressen, Chuck Harris, Gene Alexander, Herb Bielawa, Gerson Bakar, Claude and Alan, Leonard Rifas, Per and Jen, Gary Gardener, Sam Konnie, Bill Mumbach, Richard Clark, and Jake Walsh. For their help with making this book happen: Elin England, Susan Wulfekuhler, Tom Atlee, Gra Linnaea, Peggy Johnson, Melissa and Kim, Fiona McAuliffe, and L.M.

DEDICATION

TO MY DEAR WIFE ELIN. So easy to love, so hard to stay mad at. Truly the most delightful person I have ever known. How fun to find our paths continuing to unfold along such a worthwhile adventure together. Passersby enjoying a wondrous, lingering moment of existence.

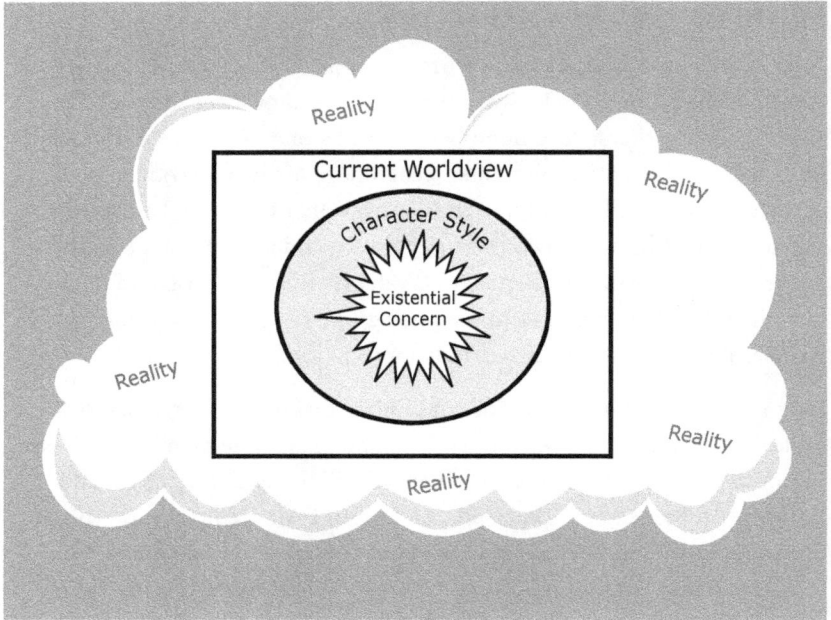

Anxiety from concern about the inescapable givens of existence exerts a near-continuous pressure on individual efforts at adaptation. Bringing one's internal needs and feelings into the external world (reality) for expression and gratification results in varying degrees of success.

Character (personality) is the sum of conditioned interpersonal strategies used to contain and mediate the interface between internal needs and feelings pressing for expression, and the external limitations and possibilities of the surrounding reality.

Worldview is considered here to be an individual's current best cognitive representation of reality, taking into account, and conditioned by, past experiences of need gratification and frustration, as well as many other factors.

—*Our destiny does not await us, we co-create it.*

Part One

Why The Book?

The current cultural momentum is:

- unsustainable
- unsatisfying
- conditioned
- fear and greed based
- changeable, but...

- Personal Growth
- Moral Maturity
- Social Evolution
- Human Potential

Part Two

Three Things

Understand the person you are talking with:

- **Section One**
  their unique
  CHARACTER STYLE

- **Section Two**
  their
  CURRENT WORLDVIEW

- **Section Three**
  which
  EXISTENTIAL CONCERN
  they are struggling with

Part Three

Techniques

You might try:

- listening
- "between the lines"
- parallel their arguments
- question assumptions
- change the context
- stick to common ground
- applaud all steps
- other ideas...

Part Four

Examples

Imagine yourself in:

- An Awkward Event
- A Workplace Conflict
- Air Travel Delay

PART ONE

Why The Book?

Introduction

"THE HOUSE IS ON FIRE!" UPON HEARING THIS, MOST PEOPLE WOULD react with a sense of alarm and respond accordingly. They'd stop what they were doing, make sure others understood the urgency of the moment, save what they could, and take steps to put out the fire. So why is it that when you talk with some people about the multiple converging challenges facing modern civilization—things like diminishing oil reserves, depletion of fisheries and freshwater, degradation and loss of topsoil, and global climate change—so many shrug it off with a "So what?"

As a kid during the 1950s, growing up in the beautiful San Francisco Bay Area, I remember feeling puzzled and unsettled at how the square, straight-lined grids of development were displacing the beautiful pastoral scenes I enjoyed viewing out the car window on leisurely rides along El Camino Real. This pleasant two-way road, lined with huge eucalyptus trees, linked a series of human-scaled towns from San Jose to San Francisco, the crown jewel at the top of the peninsula. For much of my youth, everything west of El Camino was basically an undeveloped wonderland. My friends and I would take our dogs, our sleeping bags, and our .22 rifles into the "wilderness" to camp and swim and enjoy the freedom and glories of nature. Each little town was separated by miles of beautiful, undeveloped paradise. And each had its own charming little train station. A light-rail system ran parallel to the train tracks. Not long after World War II, these tracks were torn out and this pleasant, efficient mode of transportation was eliminated.

By the mid-1960s I was beginning to understand what was happening. Huge areas of the natural world were being converted into subdivisions. Freeway systems were being set in place for a massive expansion of automobile travel. All of the quaint little towns along the peninsula between San Francisco and San Jose were rapidly becoming connected into one long strip of housing developments and commercial zones. In 1970, a college professor introduced me to Paul Erlich's *The Population Bomb*. Suddenly I had a coherent frame for understanding what I was witnessing and feeling uneasy about. It was clear

to me—and obvious to Paul Erlich and others who were paying attention—
that the burgeoning population was putting humanity on a collision course
with the Earth's finite resources. Throughout the 1970s this observation
was reinforced and further influenced by the writings of a number of other
seminal progressive and environmental authors of the day.[1] This was also, for
me, a period of shared housing situations, participation in a local food co-op,
and a growing interest and involvement in organic gardening. Like so many
of my generation, I explored a vast array of consciousness-raising experiences
in my search for self and meaning. These included workshops in the hot tubs
at Esalen Institute, group therapy at the Gestalt Institute, est, biofeedback,
meditation, personal therapy, tai chi, and many of the other "usual suspects"
typical of the 1960s quest for enlightenment. This culminated, for me, in a
formal education in psychology and a profession facilitating the personal
growth of others.

The protests and insights of the 1960s and '70s became temporarily obstructed
by a relatively brief yuppie period for me in the early 1980s, where my focus
on self-aggrandizement and starting a family took precedence, in my consciousness, over environmental and political concerns. But discernment of
the unraveling threads revealing that "the king had no clothes" kept gnawing
at me. I found myself wondering how it could be that we ended up with a
president who some considered a Lincoln-like hero, while others considered
him a second-rate actor with Alzheimer's. I could feel our civilization slip-
ping, becoming more precariously balanced, and ever more distant from and
disrespectful toward the biological underpinnings of our existence. I began
to feel too far removed from the food chain. This led, by the end of the 1980s,
to my moving to Western Oregon and "downshifting" my lifestyle.

By the time we left the S.F. Bay Area, the traffic there was horrid. People
put up with two-hour commutes each way to work. I had a psychotherapy
practice in San Francisco, and told more than one person that they would
be "cured" when they realized that it was their adaptation to a dysfunctional
society that was the problem. The pace of life was clearly unhealthy for
most people, but no one wanted to talk about it. Back then, uncomfortable
conversations about exponential economic and consumptive growth, and
how it couldn't possibly go on forever, were quickly diverted to other
topics. The dot-com phenomenon was on the edge of exploding into public

awareness and there was an excitement in the air that overtook otherwise rational people.

I now live on a small organic farm near Eugene, Oregon, with my wife and two children, where we grow a considerable amount of our own food, endeavor to live simply, develop local community, and spend less time in cars and malls. We are much less engaged in the hectic pace of pop-culture consumerism. We have no TV. Our carbon footprint, for a family of four, is less than that of one average person in North America. And our quality of life is amazingly high. Many unsustainable compromises are still made daily. Life is not always easy, but it is, in many ways, better and more fulfilling. It is from this vantage point that my perspective in this book has taken shape.

Eventually, as it seemed increasingly obvious to me that multiple, converging challenges were becoming more dire (e.g., rising levels of persistent toxic pollution, diminishing natural resources, economic instability, questionable elections, unjustifiable wars, mounting evidence of global climate change, etc.), I found myself wondering why people were *still* not talking about these issues. This frustration was exacerbated by 9-11 and the invasion of Iraq, after which I found myself uncomfortably on the "other side" of conversations with people I thought I knew. I began to feel concerned about the media-driven divisiveness that seemed to be gripping our nation. All around me, people were being polite instead of authentic. But the issues we were facing required thoughtful engagement and dialogue. What the heck was going on? This eventually led to my looking more deeply at how it is we arrive at such different perspectives while living in the same world at the same time.

After years of frustration and reflection, I decided to write this book. Not because I have all the answers. In fact, I struggle with this. I found that I'm not always very good at communicating across the divides in my life. I find myself not listening very well, not communicating very effectively, and not feeling closer and more connected to people after our conversation. I end up feeling discouraged instead of hopeful about our collective ability to move forward together, as a society, in a mutually beneficial way. So part of the reason for writing this book has been to organize my best thinking about this problem in one place. It's been a way to bring together those ideas that I have found useful in my attempts at dialogue across the divide. Also, it is my hope that maybe others who, like myself, are concerned about these divides, might find something helpful here for their everyday struggles in this area.

My hope is to help those who understand, for example, such concepts as "overshoot and collapse," to be able to communicate their concerns effectively with their families, friends, neighbors, and co-workers in a respectful manner that offers a rational view that, perhaps, differs from what is typically espoused by pop-culture media. I want to encourage the collective questioning of whether the current cultural promotion of unbridled consumption and perpetual exponential growth is a reasonable way to proceed, as a global civilization, in the twenty-first century. So yes, part of my goal is to spread the message of sustainability as opposed to perpetuating a global socio-economic system that is destined to fail as a result of its own inherent structural flaws.

Thirty years of involvement with psychoanalytic inquiry have led me to question why seemingly intelligent, well-functioning, well-meaning individuals engage in such maladaptive behavior. If you said to someone, "Your house is on fire," most people would pay attention and take more or less immediate and appropriate actions. But alas, when you point out to the majority of the population that their water supply is being poisoned, the air they breathe is unhealthy, the soils, forests, and fisheries which supply their basic sustenance are being degraded and eliminated; they somehow fail to respond adaptively. You can present people with data that clearly demonstrate the rate at which we are destroying the biosphere upon which we depend as a species. And they might even agree that it is important. But it still doesn't seem to result in significant changes of behavior.

Why?

Because, as I intend to illustrate in this book, there are, among other factors, numerous psychological resistances (ego defense mechanisms) that perpetuate unsustainable behavior.

The combination of Jared Diamond's[2] thoughtful list of what people say when confronted with the notion that civilizations can and do collapse from environmental degradation, along with George Lakoff's[3] penetrating deconstruction of the values-laden subtext of people's communications, reminded me to listen with the "analytic ear" I had honed during my years as a professional. I became curious about the factors that could lead people to overlook such important data as the fact that their civilization, perhaps even their species, was in danger. Aside from the numerous socio-economic and political explanations, which I am unqualified to evaluate, I began to examine what other factors—those of an individual psychological nature—might explain such a lack of response, and what's needed to address the maladaptive aspects of human experience that perpetuate unsustainable behavior.

When talking across a divide, there are Three Things I believe we need to understand and keep in mind about the person we are speaking with: 1) the person's individual psychological *character style* with its unique constellation of ego defenses; 2) their *current worldview* which gives us clues as to what will resonate with them as positive and plausible, as well as what is likely to turn them off and make them discount our message without even hearing it; and 3) which *existential concern* has been aroused by our (bad news) message about the coming adaptations that will likely be required.

Understanding these Three Things empowers us to devise a communicative strategy that: 1) gets past (through) their conditioned defensive layer without snagging; 2) appeals to their current view of the world with an implicit invitation to consider expanding their view to include more of ours; and 3) soothes any existential angst stirred up by their consideration of the "bad news."

So, why the book? Because I felt it was time to add my voice to the dialogue about how we might collectively navigate our way forward as a civilization, to learn how to stop arguing over differences and deliberate together in a way that allows our highest truths to prevail, and to encourage us to learn how to move together, in unison, as a global community, with cooperation, compassion, and joy.

Peace in the world cannot be achieved so long as we remain divisive within our own communities. We must learn to reach out across the divides to those who are unlike us—person by person, situation by situation. It's been said, if you want to make peace, talk with your enemies—if you want to feel good, talk with your friends. This book is about learning how to consider all inhabitants of Earth as friends in a global community, even if we disagree, and find ways to work together to sustain that connection.

---

[1] *Steps to an Ecology of Mind* by Gregory Bateson, *The Limits to Growth* by Donella Meadows et al., *Small is Beautiful* by E.F. Schumacher, *Silent Spring* by Rachel Carson, *The Structure of Scientific Revolutions* by Thomas Kuhn, *Diet for a Small Planet* by Francis Moore Lappe, and many others of this ilk.

[2] Diamond, J. (2005).

[3] Lakoff, G. (2004).

DISCLAIMER

Please note: The characterizations of individuals in this book are inescapably biased and distorted by my own personal anxieties, psychological defenses, and worldview. They are also heavily influenced by my psychoanalytic training and may sometimes have a harsh, uncompassionate, cynical, or belittling tone. It is not my intention to imply any superiority on my part, or inferiority in anyone else. Rather, I have attempted to "raise to awareness" those aspects of human functioning that can sometimes present difficult impediments to effective communication.

My hope is that this book will be used to generate dialogue and perhaps lines of research for further inquiry about how these psychological factors fit together and what role they play in the sustainability movement. This book is my attempt to formulate an initial coherent conceptualization of how these variables affect our collective navigation, as a society, in the face of multiple converging challenges.

To what degree is conscious social evolution possible? I don't know. To what degree can we override our base instincts of aggression and greed in the face of threats to our survival as a species? I'm not sure. But these questions are, I think, important to ask and to talk about.

I don't consider myself to be "the expert" in these matters. I'm just beginning to notice how these pieces of the puzzle might fit together and might be addressed. I welcome the responses, observations, challenges, and refinements of others in thinking about this potentially important aspect of collective life. I haven't yet identified, let alone tested with any scientific methodology, all of the dos and don'ts for communicating effectively with every character type and worldview. My hope is that this book will serve as a first step in that direction.

Astute readers should have no problem identifying the inconsistencies of my "progressive" logic, or the arrogance of my mean-green worldview. That is my current stance in life, as of this writing. The approach to collective deliberation that I am proposing here will benefit from the contributions of multiple perspectives as we all try to reach across the divides in our everyday lives to find the common ground and shared values that will illuminate our best path forward together.

PART ONE: WHY THE BOOK?

The Current Cultural Momentum is Unsustainable

A GROWING NUMBER OF SCIENTISTS AND ACADEMICS AGREE THAT THE exponentially expanding global economy is on a collision course with the planet's unyielding ecological limits. A host of looming problems associated with the continuing expansion of the current industrial paradigm will increasingly constrain options for future human development, health, and well-being[1].

Air pollution, diminishing fresh water supplies, loss and degradation of topsoil, enormous amounts of waste, a build-up of persistent toxins in the food chain and the biosphere, reduction of biological diversity, global climate change, depletion of non-renewable energy sources upon which our current civilization depends, increasing economic inequality, and other converging challenges have led many to recognize that the current cultural momentum is not sustainable. We cannot continue to erode the biological underpinnings of our very existence and hope to thrive as a species.

The Millennium Ecosystem Assessment[2], an undertaking commissioned by the United Nations that integrates the efforts of 1,350 researchers from 95 countries in a peer-reviewed process, represents the most comprehensive data, to date, for understanding our relationship as a species to the global biological systems we depend on and are a part of.

Their detailed examination of the interconnection between the effects of human behavior on ecosystems, and the effects of ecosystems on human well-being concluded that "Humans are fully dependent on Earth's ecosystems and the services they provide, such as food, clean water, disease regulation, climate regulation, and others. Changes in ecosystem services influence all components of human well-being, including the basic material needs for a good life, health, good social relations, security, and freedom of choice and action. The degradation of ecosystem services often causes significant harm to human well-being. Over the past fifty years, humans have changed ecosystems more rapidly and extensively than in any comparable period of time in human history, largely to meet rapidly growing demands for food, fresh water, timber, fiber, and fuel. This has resulted in a substantial and largely irreversible loss in the diversity of life on Earth. Gains have been achieved at growing costs in the form of the degradation of many ecosystem services, increased risk of nonlinear changes, and the exacerbation of poverty for some groups of people. These problems, unless addressed, will substantially diminish the benefits that future generations obtain from ecosystems."

"Ecologically unsustainable use of ecosystem services raises the potential for serious and irreversible ecological change. Ecosystem changes may occur on such a large scale as to have a catastrophic effect upon the economic, social and political processes upon which social stability, human wellbeing and good health are dependent."[3] "Even wealthy populations cannot be fully insulated from the degradation of ecosystem services."[2] "In the long run, rich people do not secure their own interests and those of their children. They merely buy themselves the privilege of being the last to starve. Our unsustainable consumption means that the First World could not continue for long on its present course, even if the Third World didn't exist and weren't trying to catch up to us."[4]

Much more could be said about the environmental challenges we face as a species. But it is not within the scope of this book, nor the purpose of this book, to detail and document the various ecological tragedies that are playing out. It is assumed that the reader has a basic understanding and concern regarding the ongoing assaults to the earth's biosphere that threaten human health and well-being. If further information is of interest or required for debate, then a review of the data presented in the sources referenced here should leave no doubt about the validity of such concerns.

---

[1] Brown, L. (2006, 2001); Daly, H. (1990); Diamond, J. (2005); Ehrlich, P. and Ehrlich, A. (2004); EPA. (2007); Lorey, D. (2003); Meadows et al. (2005); Millennium Ecosystem Assessment. (2005); Pimm, S. (2001); Smil, V. (2003); Union of Concerned Scientists. (1992); United Nations. (1998, 2002); Wackernagel et al. (2002); Watson et al. (2001); World Bank. (2001a & b); Worldwatch Institute. (2004); Worldwatch Institute. (1984–2005).

[2] Millennium Ecosystem Assessment. (2005).

[3] Ecosystems and Human Health. (2007).

[4] Diamond, J. (2005).

The Current Cultural Momentum is Unsatisfying

Quality of Life versus Standard of Living

FOR ALL OUR GREAT WEALTH AS A NATION, WE'RE NOT REALLY ALL THAT happy. Not really. Cheerful? Perhaps. Cultural conditioning encourages it. Distracted, indulged and entertained? You bet. But happy? No. Not really. Not most of us. In fact, our hectic lives leave little room to even reflect on the matter. Our frantic pursuit of *more* keeps us outpacing ourselves under the illusion that we can fill that gnawing hole in us with "stuff"—more stuff, better stuff, the *right* stuff. But alas, the joy of acquisition is short-lived and our dissatisfaction spurs us on in an endless hollow pursuit.

A number of authors[1] in recent years, wondering about this phenomenon, have arrived at a similar conclusion—more money and more stuff doesn't necessarily result in more happiness. In fact, the correlation drops off rather dramatically shortly beyond the point that one's basic physical needs (food, shelter, safety) are being met. After that point, our lives are not really *better*, but simply more cluttered and complicated with more things to maintain, insure, dust, store, move, worry about, try to find time to enjoy, and so forth. Actual "quality of life" by a number of measures (see sidebar on page 17) is not enhanced to any significant degree.

In analyzing why having "more" no longer makes us happy, many are beginning to challenge the sacred underlying philosophical stance of our current industrial-growth economy; that is, economist Adam Smith's[2] notion that if we all just pursue our own self-interest in the most selfish, greedy, and aggressive manner, we'll co-generate wealth that benefits us all in a never-ending upward spiral. This theory works, up to a point. It has, indeed, worked beautifully to lift the standard of living of many industrialized nations. This has occurred, however, at a great cost to many "poor" parts of the world, a fact that is not often acknowledged.

But what is *also* true is that the self-interest approach worked *better* in Adam Smith's era—when resources were many and people were fewer—than it is working *now*, when resources are dwindling and there are so darn many of us. Perhaps a reevaluation of our tack is in order. The continued pursuit of ever-higher levels of material consumption is not only no longer improving our lives, it is certain to impoverish future generations and make them resent our short-sighted greed and narcissistic indulgence at their expense. It could even jeopardize our survival as a species.

The idea of limits to growth is not a popular one among our current mainstream pundits and politicians. It keeps getting spun as an attempt to sell a grim, joyless life. But that doesn't have to be the case at all. The emerging culture and consciousness of sustainable living carries with it a number of innovative ways of living that, in fact, add richness, meaning, and fulfillment to the lives of those experimenting with new options. Not everybody needs a huge house or a new car or the latest electronic gadget in order to feel good about themselves and to enjoy their lives. Especially if it means they are putting up with a long commute, longer hours at the office, and yet another fast-food dinner on-the-run to pay for it. Not everyone buys into the neo-liberal mandate to "grow the economy." Many are starting to recognize that while the economy continues to grow, most of us are not really getting richer—not significantly anyway—and that how we are currently living isn't even *close* to sustainable. As our vast oil inheritance continues to be squandered, so goes the wealth of our global civilization. In fact, at the moment, we seem to be spending an enormous amount of our collective wealth and resources fighting over the remaining resources that we could be learning to share and use wisely. Maybe, after all, we're not the pinnacle and end-all of evolution on Earth. Maybe we need to look beyond Darwin's last page to see our possible collective fate. Just do the math—what's the likelihood that the billions of people emerging into the consumer class in China and India are going to be able to enjoy the same standard of living as current North Americans, Europeans, and Japanese? Really. Where are all of these natural resources going to come from? There simply aren't enough on this finite planet. Period. Something's gotta give. And in all likelihood, it's going to have to be *us*.

But learning how to enjoy a higher quality of life with less material throughput needn't necessarily be a *bad* thing. In fact, it might turn out to be quite wonderful. It might mean that we finally get to slow down, spend time with our families and friends, get to know our neighbors, share a garden, eat home-cooked meals again, work closer to home, get more exercise by walking and bicycling instead of commuting so far in cars. Yes, this involves an adjustment in what we've thought of as "progress" and "the good life." Yes, it's going to involve a change in consciousness. Because the health of the biosphere in which we live—the air we breathe, the water we drink, the food we eat—is not only the biological basis of our economy, it's also directly related to our *quality of life* and well-being. Do we really want to "grow the economy" at our own expense? Isn't the economy *our* creation? Isn't the economy supposed to serve *us*, humanity? Or are we here to serve some abstract, monolithic notion of "the economy" as though it were a living entity with a higher purpose and more legitimate needs and rights than our own? The economy wins, we lose. Who made *that* up? Who *is* pulling the strings behind the curtain? These are important, critical questions that we should all be asking. However, many of them are beyond the scope of this book.

Our focus needs to be on learning how to communicate about these issues and concerns across the philosophical and psychological divides in our daily lives. It's up to us to stop asking each other "What'dya get at the store?" and start focusing on "How is life for you these days?" We need to start questioning with each other whether *more* is better or not, and just how much *is* enough. Our conversations need to acknowledge that while GDP (Gross Domestic Product, the total of economic activity or money spent) has gone up, life satisfaction, for most people, has not. Alcoholism, bankruptcy, divorce, depression all seem impervious to the accumulation of more stuff.

So how is it that we became so focused on the idea that the accumulation of more wealth would make us happy? Why is it that Forbes magazine's "richest Americans" are no happier than the Pennsylvania Amish? The short answers include: profitable media-driven consumerism (see the next chapter), and the fact that we basically have taken a good idea (generating collective wealth) and kept doing it (increasing material acquisition) way beyond its useful phase. Ramping up consumerism no longer fits our current global circumstances. We've gone past the point of diminishing returns to where consumerism has become detrimental to our well-being and is endangering the prospects of future generations. McKibben[3] characterizes this mistake as an all-too-common error in thinking that those who are addicted often resort to "If two beers made me feel good, then ten should make me feel *really* good." Oy, what a hangover!

Okay, so we've gone a little too far in the wrong direction—a direction that no longer brings us what we want. All right then, let's take a moment—a very brief moment because the clock is ticking—and reevaluate our situation and use our collective power of self-direction to consider a different path. Let's put aside our apathy, inertia, habitual momentums, and cynicism, grieve our lost dreams of endlessly increasing wealth, and consciously evolve together into a more sustainable and fulfilling global community. We can do it. We can choose it. We can co-create it. There's no law of the land or law of the universe that says we cannot change directions at any moment that we choose.

But we need to begin envisioning together what that new world will look like and how we can actually begin shifting our lives in that direction. What conveniences and comforts do we fear will need to be sacrificed at the altar of sustainability? What would be acceptable? What wouldn't? What alternatives exist? We need to be having these discussions among ourselves in a way that leads to meaningful change.

That is the purpose of this book—to promote productive dialogue about difficult issues with people who don't see things the same way we do. It bears repeating, because this is likely to be one part of the "bad news" of sustainability that most people don't want to hear (but that we are all going to have to deal with sooner or later), that *progress in advancing our quality of life and well-being is not always going to be synonymous with maximizing convenience or comfort.* But what's also true is that the oncoming changes and adaptations that will be required may do more for increasing the joy and meaning in our lives than consumerism *ever* did.

If a truly rich and successful global community is to be judged by the happiness of its citizens and its generosity toward future generations, rather than by how much stuff it accumulates, then a reevaluation of what it means to be successful and rich is in order. Traditionally, we have relied on GDP per capita as a measure of society's success. Yet this measure not only promotes unnecessary consumption, but lumps together factors which detract from quality of life with those that enhance it. GDP also fails to measure unpaid activities that contribute to quality of life, such as parental child care, doing your own gardening, or making love. In the old view, a person dying of lung cancer from smoking cigarettes or someone who gets drunk and causes a lethal car accident makes a "positive" contribution to the GDP. These individuals stimulate economic activity through hospital bills, lawyer bills, funeral expenses, and so forth, as well as their consumption of tobacco, alcohol, and automobile-related expenses. Are they good citizens? According to the old paradigm, yes. They have helped generate wealth from which we all benefit. But do they add to our quality of life? Surely we can find better ways.

As we begin to rethink "the good life," we can find many examples of activities and ways of living that many, perhaps most, people seem to inherently value. It's not rocket science. We just need to look around and notice our own sources of genuine pleasure—rather than seeking escape, diversion, or entertainment. It's been a long-standing observation that people on their deathbeds are unlikely to wish they had spent another hour at the office. People these days are increasingly rushed and have little time for themselves, their families, friends, and neighbors. And yet this is something that most people would like more of—time to just hang out. "Time poverty" has clearly accompanied the rise of affluence. What would it be like to "downshift" to a simpler, less stressful life? We need to be asking ourselves this.

Assuming the basics (food, shelter, personal safety) are met (and granted they are not for far too many people), social connections come pretty quickly to the foreground for most people. Good social relations, family life, and social cohesion in one's community are highly valued aspects of a high quality of life—far more than frivolous material possessions. Most people love getting together in large groups to celebrate and enjoy each other's company. Humans are social animals.

Outdoor markets with local street vendors, free concerts in the park, picnics, family reunions, parties with old friends, church socials, and holiday meals are things that we can see with our own eyes, and intuitively know, that people genuinely enjoy, that contribute to a high quality of life, and that most of us would gladly trade a few hours at work for more of. Incorporating more of these types of social richness into our lives is possible, but involves a shift in priorities as well as policy and education initiatives to back it. It means moving from an infrastructure of consumption to an infrastructure of well-being and real enjoyment of life.

Research shows us that people who have strong social connections are happier and healthier. Social networks build a sense of trust, individual and community resilience, increased reciprocity, information sharing, and economic activity. Yet we continue to fragment as a society. We've gone from front-porch sitting and visiting with neighbors, to each separate family in its own house sitting around a television, to each person in the house sitting in their own room staring at their own computer. This is *not* making us happier.

---

[1] Durning. (1992); Gardner and Assadourian. (2004); McKibben. (2007); Prescott-Allen. (2001).

[2] Smith, A. (1776).

[3] McKibben, B. (2007).

MEASURING QUALITY OF LIFE

There have been a number of alternative measures developed in recent years to begin providing more context for quality of life and well-being factors than the traditional GDP measure accounts for. These include:

- The Genuine Progress Indicator

- The Human Development Index

- The Living Planet Index

- The Wellbeing Index

The Wellbeing Index is noteworthy for its comprehensiveness. It uses 87 indicators to measure human and ecological well-being—ranging from life expectancy and school enrollment rates to the extent of deforestation and levels of carbon emissions. These indicators can help us identify those areas in which quality of life is suffering. Values from the array of indicators are standardized and summed into a single score for ease of comparison across 180 countries.

The results are revealing: some two thirds of the world's people live in countries with a bad or poor rating for human well-being. Only Norway, Denmark, and Finland receive the highest of the five rating levels. Meanwhile, countries with a poor or bad environmental rating cover almost half of Earth's land area. And no country receives a good environmental rating.

The Index's separate measures of human and environmental well-being help crystallize an ideal development goal: to improve people's lives with the least possible environmental impact. Indeed, the Index reveals that people's basic needs can be met with a range of environmental price tags. How a nation meets its development goals is as important as whether it meets them.

17

PART ONE: WHY THE BOOK?

The Current Cultural Momentum is Conditioned

The Role of the Media

ANIMALS CAN BE TRAINED TO BEHAVE IN WAYS THAT ARE NOT NATURAL for them—not part of their innate behavioral repertoire. Tigers, for instance, don't routinely jump through flaming hoops. They run from fire. Primary reinforcement (e.g., food or pain) can be used, methodically, to incrementally shape the behavior of animals to perform all sorts of tricks. Humans are animals too, and our behavior can be similarly shaped by the reinforcement contingencies in our lives. We all respond to pleasure and pain in predictable ways—by moving toward and opening to pleasure, and moving away from and tightening against pain.

Secondary reinforcers are those which have become associated with a primary reinforcer. A starving person (or animal) can quite easily be manipulated to perform behaviors for food—a primary reinforcer. People living on the edge, those who are within a paycheck of being homeless, are often quite willing to accept demeaning employment and paper money (a secondary reinforcer) in order to ensure a roof over their heads and their next few meals. To some degree, we've all been trained to jump through hoops for secondary reinforcement (a paycheck) which can be exchanged for primary reinforcers (food, shelter, etc.).

One can increase the likelihood that certain behaviors will be repeated by applying "positive" reinforcement, that is, by giving rewards such as food (primary) or money (secondary). Or, one can increase the likelihood of those same behaviors being repeated by *removing* some sort of pain associated with *not* performing the desired behavior. This subtractive form of reinforcement is referred to by behavioral psychologists as "negative" reinforcement. By taking away something that is causing pain, you increase the likelihood that the behavior will be performed again. Positive, here, means applying stimulus. Negative means subtracting or removing stimulus.

If I twist your arm, or strap you to a chair and run a painful electric current through your body until you say "Uncle," you will learn to turn off the painful stimulus by saying the correct word. This is how addictions are formed. I feel uneasy inside. I take this or that drug. I feel less uneasy inside. I feel relieved and that feels good. The painful electric current has temporarily stopped. Taking the drug has just been reinforced by turning off the pain. The likelihood that I will do it again has increased. I do it again. It works again. Pretty soon I'm doing it all the time without thinking. A habit is a behavior that has gone from consciously performing it to unconsciously performing it. An addiction is something that is hard to stop doing even though it is, ultimately, self-defeating.

Television[1] is an addiction for many people. It fits the criteria set forth by the American Psychiatric Association for addiction. Yes, it's a great source for information about our culture and has all of those other arguments in its favor. But for many people, watching TV is also a behavior that shuts off the pain of their daily lives. It becomes a maladaptive dependency used for escape, to avoid rather than address the sources of discontent in their lives. People rarely admit that they watch more TV than they consciously intend to. Yet many have experienced unsuccessful attempts to reduce their viewing. They realize that it takes time away from other, more productive, activities as well as from enjoyable social and recreational pursuits. Yet they find themselves "glued to the set" despite this recognition of the problems it causes them. This sounds like an addictive behavior to me.

What makes television so addictive? The alluring, dazzling audio-visual spectacle itself is "mesmerizing" in a matter of seconds. Watch how people's eyes glaze over almost immediately when they lock on to the television set in a room. Franz Mesmer (of eighteenth-century "animal magnetism" fame) led the way to what is now known as clinical hypnosis—a deep state of relaxation coupled with heightened suggestibility. Suggestibility is a key component of hypnotic trance. Those who are more suggestible are more easily hypnotized. This is a clinical fact. Post-hypnotic "suggestions" are implanted in the receptive subconscious while under the induced trance state which, presumably, when one is awake again, will be helpful in changing targeted habits such as smoking, over-eating, and so forth. Television, especially commercials, with a flurry of fast-paced high-interest images and alarming sounds, generates a trance-state that is virtually impossible for most, if not all, to resist. Within about thirty seconds, our conscious attention cannot keep up with the on-slaught of stimuli, we suspend disbelief, and fall into the trance of suggestibil-ity. We go with the program. Our brain waves actually shift from beta (alert, awake, analytic thinking) to alpha (relaxed, daydreaming, suggestible) which is what turns off the painful electricity of our daily lives. We zone out in front of the tube, get our attention off of our worries, and enjoy the break from our overactive mind. There we sit—blank stare, jaw dropped open, taking it in—just how the advertisers want us. Blissfully transported to a different reality, their reality. Open to *their* images and messages being implanted deeply into our subconscious minds. We let go of our own thinking and take in theirs. They'll tell us what we want, how we should be, what will make us happy.

We turn off the pain by zoning out, and it works. Television puts us into a receptive alpha trance with heightened suggestibility and it feels good. That's why it's so addictive. But the unexamined consequences to our lives, and the lives of so many others, are what we need to be talking about. For without becoming conscious of this effect, a self-defeating unconscious habit keeps us in our place in a system that feeds off of our passivity. Media critics spend years training themselves to see through this trance and understand (and use) the mechanics of this process of induction.

Noam Chomsky (1989, 1992) has a lot to say about how the media are used by powerful corporations, representing affluent elite interests, to create "necessary illusions" in order to "manufacture consent" among educated, otherwise-well-meaning people in democratic societies to go along with atrocities such as profitable wars and the exploitation of other nation's resources, with a sense of privilege and entitlement under the banners of "national interest" and "spreading democracy." Yes, the media are complicit in manufacturing consent to go to war. This type of thought control (propagan-da) has been used by powerful regimes throughout history, and is now used by corporate-sponsored media, to shape a view of world events that favors the dominance and perpetuation of the ruling class, while it elicits compli-ance from the hegemonic empires' populace. "Propaganda is to a democracy what violence is to a dictatorship—a way to control the masses." This subtle manipulation of perceived-reality is accomplished by the media's control over *which* topics are selected for coverage, *where* the emphasis in a media presentation is placed, *how* the issues are framed, and *what* information is filtered out. The media determine (limit) the boundaries of the debate. They control and shape public opinion with the programming they offer. They present a view of democracy that favors the status quo power structure for the elite, while it distracts, diverts, marginalizes and controls the masses "for their own good."

Any attempt to broaden the scope of issues discussed to include those that might actually be of interest to the people whose lives are affected by the decisions being made gets excluded or, at best, minimal coverage. About 20% of the population—those with higher education—the professionals, the decision-makers, corporate CEOs, policy crafters, agenda-setters, and so forth, are deeply indoctrinated in the social-political-economic mindset of the affluent elites. They are invited into the ruling class with substantial inducements and rewards of power, influence, authority, affluence, prestige, access, and privilege. Gaining the consent of the upper class is essential to perpetuating the current system. They must also be constrained, however, through institutional structures to implement the agenda that serves the hierarchy of power.

The remaining 80% of the population all-too-often simply falls in line. They have clearly ingested the "suggestion" that it is *their* destiny to follow orders, to not think or pay attention to the decisions being made that affect their lives (and which they end up paying for with their labor). They are all-too-easily pacified with a beer and a sitcom or a sports game. The corporate-sponsored media get what they want—they deliver suggestible audiences to advertisers. In many cases, the corporations advertising the products are part of the same conglomerate that owns the media running the ads. How's *that* for a closed-loop? Go to work, produce, pay taxes, consume, die. There you have it—life in a nutshell.

One way in which the current corporate-dominated media negatively affect citizens' understanding of important issues is by reducing complex issues to short, simplified sound bites. Chomsky points out how the mandate of "concision" (conciseness) permeates commercial media. In television and radio programs, for example, the message has to basically fit between two commercial breaks. Print media articles are best kept to about 600 words, the amount an average person can read in one sitting on the toilet.

One of the effects of concision is that it's hard to encompass large concepts with enough background and supporting evidence in such a short amount of time or few words. So those with urgent messages end up having to resort to emotional appeals, slogans, and sound bites. Not enough time for depth of exposition or critical analysis. The result is that truly innovative ideas end up sounding shallow and eccentric. If you go beyond conventional thinking, the format of the media simply doesn't allow for the necessary examination of context and methodology. To some degree, in-depth analysis of issues is the role of academia. But this is why researchers and academics say one thing about global climate change, for example, and the pop-culture media (until very recently) say another. Fair and balanced isn't either unless you take the time to examine the facts in depth. Our sources of information don't have to be about opinions or pundits. We can require programming that examines the evidence, seeks the truth, and presents rational understandings to guide the course of civilization.

The media have been reduced to rehashing the same old neo-liberal mantras about "spreading democracy," "growing the economy," "trickle down," and so forth. Most people are so entranced by the delivery of the message—"Cool graphics dude!"—that they just nod and go along thinking everything is going to work out just fine—"Oh well, my personal finances are doing pretty good." Meanwhile, valid dissenting views remain unnoticed by the masses. They don't get air time because they can't be reduced to sound bites without seeming like eccentric bumpersticker ideas. The people who try to advance those ideas end up looking foolish and are easily shot down and dismissed by the smug follow-up quips of the hosts who frame them. (To the camera: "Well, all right then, *that* was different." To their co-host: "I don't know, Tom, do you really think that blah, blah, blah is to blame?" To the camera: "Stay tuned, we'll be right back after these messages.") This has the same dampening effect as using the term "conspiracy theory" to discourage and discredit valid investigation of suspected corruption.

There are some who criticize television as a subtle, invasive form of social training and control with problems that go beyond programming and advertising—that by its very nature, television (and other technologies) can be detrimental to humanity. Mander[2] asserts that the medium of television not only entrances the viewer, it also displaces other important forms of thinking and knowing with the relatively shallow thoughts and images of program producers. It separates people from nature and conditions children to accept a fast-paced, high-technology life as normal. He doesn't accept the premise that all technologies are neutral and that their affects on humanity—good or bad—depend upon how they are used. Some technologies, he says, have inherent qualities which make them *not* neutral, for example nuclear energy. It may *also* be that humanity lacks the moral maturity to handle potentially destructive technologies even though we have the intellect to invent them. Mander challenges our passivity about accepting new technologies as inevitable in our lives and encourages public discussion about the potential costs—social, environmental, political—before blithely accepting new technologies as "necessary" or "beneficial" to well-being, based on the claims of those (advertisers) who stand to profit from the uncritical, wide-scale adoption of a new technology. Technologies such as television and computers, he asserts, extend corporate control and promote wanton consumption of natural resources. While they may seem harmless and useful, they can also serve to condition a populace for the emergence of non-democratic social control. The insidious manner in which these technologies make inroads into people's lives, replacing human-to-human interaction with human-to-machine interactions, is worth keeping an eye on.

So, what it comes down to is this: whether we are going to individually and collectively go along with (i.e., condone with our silence) the cultural trance that promotes excessive, unconscious, habitual consumption at the expense of other people and the environment, or whether we are going to unplug the TV (so to speak) and unplug from the consumer culture and the conditioning forces in our lives, broaden our news sources and information streams, sharpen our critical-thinking skills, and have authentic face-to-face discussions about those issues that really matter. Are we going to be compliant citizens of empire—have a beer, watch a game—or are we going to co-create a global community based on cooperation, compassion, generosity, truth, and sustainability? Awakening from the cultural trance is possible and it's happening to an increasing number of people—right now. A transnational people's movement is arising to reclaim self-determination. We're all invited. Bring your friends and neighbors.

---

[1] Television is taking all the heat in this chapter. But, many of the arguments made here pertain to *all* forms of mediated reality, where the media-consumer's view of the world is slanted by the "lens" of the media-producer and the medium itself. Thus, all media—print, radio, internet blogs, whatever—have essentially the same effect of providing a necessarily biased and limited point of view which the media-producer thinks, for one reason or another, is important.

[2] Mander, J. (1978, 1992).

DIALOGUE AND COLLECTIVE INTELLIGENCE

Tom Atlee's *The Tao of Democracy: Using Co-Intelligence to Create a World that Works for All* (2003) is an excellent resource on the role of collective intelligence and the use of innovative dialogue methods for the democratic transformation of society. It contains numerous useful examples of how to generate co-created wisdom and explains why "we need greater collective intelligence than our democracy is able to deliver in its current form." He illuminates the need for a holistic, democratic political process (not just ideology) that can call forth the "voice-of-the-whole" and empower any group, community, or society to reflect on itself and benefit from its own collective wisdom.

He encourages conscious cultural evolution—the wise co-creation of a better future—via processes that effectively enhance our ability to collaboratively think, feel, and dream together. Co-intelligence, defined as "what intelligence would look like if we took wholeness, interconnectedness, and co-creativity seriously" and "accessing the wisdom of the whole on behalf of the whole" arises, Atlee demonstrates, from processes like the Citizen Deliberative Council, to which he gives much attention. The basic thesis is that, "Given a supportive structure and resources, diverse ordinary people can work together to reach common ground, creating wise and deliberate policy that reflects the highest public interest." This involves committing a small, demographically diverse, representative sampling of the population to a time-limited process where they research an issue, engage in dialogue, deliberate on their needs, and deliver viable solutions that integrate and go beyond seemingly opposed points of view. The creative integration of diversity results in wise, collective self-governance.

Atlee's description of "resonant intelligence"—intelligence that grows stronger and fuller as it resonates with other sources or forms of intelligence, an aspect of collective intelligence in group settings—is compelling and accurately fits with my experience and observations.

From these understandings, many useful tools are offered that can be experimented with and applied to all sorts of situations where people would benefit from having greater decision-making power over the decisions that affect their lives.

His Web site co-intelligence.org describes how these powerful conversational tools could be institutionalized in our democratic politics and governance, generating a "wise democracy."

PREFERENCE VOTING (IRV)

Preference Voting, also called Instant Runoff Voting (IRV), offers a viable and more democratic alternative to the two most widely used voting systems in America today, namely "plurality elections" and "two-round runoff elections."

In plurality voting, candidates can win with less than a majority when there are more than two candidates running for an office. In contrast, Preference Voting (IRV) elects a majority candidate while still allowing voters to support a candidate who is not a front runner—their preferred candidate.

Preference Voting (IRV) accommodates multiple candidates in single-seat races and ensures that a "spoiler" effect will not result in an undemocratic outcome. It allows all voters to vote for their favorite candidate without fear of wasting their vote or helping elect their least favorite candidate, and it ensures that the winner enjoys true support from a majority of voters.

How does it work?

On their ballots, voters rank the various candidates as their first choice, second choice, third choice, and so forth. The ballots are submitted and the first choice candidates are counted. If one of the candidates does not receive a clear majority of votes on the first counting of the ballots, then a series of "runoff" counts are conducted.

In the first runoff round, the candidate who previously received the fewest first-place ballots is eliminated. If a voter's first choice candidate is eliminated, then their second choice becomes their new "top choice." If your first choice is eliminated, then your second choice still counts.

All ballots are then recounted, with each ballot still contributing just one vote for each voter's favorite candidate who is still in contention. Voters who chose the eliminated candidate are now voting for their second-choice candidate, while all other voters continue supporting their top candidate. This process of elimination and recount continues until one candidate receives a clear majority.

The benefits of IRV include ensuring majority rule. The candidate supported by the most people wins the election (in contrast to plurality voting). The winning candidate has maximum popular support. IRV also tends to decrease negative campaigning and saves money by avoiding the need for primary and costly runoff elections (which have notoriously low voter turnout). ▶

27

Preference Voting (IRV) also tends to broaden the public dialogue by welcoming more than two points of view, and promotes positive, issue-based campaigns, since candidates will be motivated to seek second and third choice votes among the populace. It also increases voter turnout, research has shown, by giving voters more choices. Exit polls show that voters prefer IRV to more traditional voting systems, and have no difficulty understanding how it works. And, it's easy and inexpensive to implement.

An increasing number of government races, universities, and organizations are utilizing Preference Voting (IRV) because of these benefits. It has been used for decades in various places in the U.S. and around the world as a simple, common-sense, cost-saving reform that improves the democratic process.

Preference Voting (Instant Runoff Voting) is a forward step in the evolution of democracy.

For more information see www.fairvote.org

The Current Cultural Momentum is Fear-and-Greed Based

FEAR AND GREED ARE AMONG THE MOST BASIC, PRIMITIVE, UNEVOLVED MODES of human functioning. Fear underlies many other emotions. We get angry rather than feel afraid. Under our sadness is the fear that we are incapable and that life is hopeless. Greed and hoarding have probably served us well, as an adaptive strategy, during harsh times; those who grasped and defended survived.

But it might be that we are entering a new phase of human development, a phase where vicious competition for dwindling resources may actually be detrimental to our survival as a species. We could end up killing each other over the table scraps of civilization's excesses. Or, we could begin to learn how to recognize, open to, accept, and manage more maturely our underlying fears and impulses to grab.

Fear and greed often result in unattractive, undignified behavior. Compassion, generosity, and the acceptance of uncertainty in life, on the other hand, can lead us to a remarkably poised presence. How can we continue to fall for the illusion that fear and greed will lead us to happiness, rather than a bunker-cold, false sense of security? How long until we recognize the warm, restful pleasure of having "enough" in our lives, rather than constantly scrambling for "more?" When will we understand that until the poorest children on the planet are fed and educated, world peace cannot become our destiny as a species? Moving toward a more compassionate, generous, and sustainable society needn't be difficult. Yes, there's a lot to do, but it really involves less *doing* and more *being*—being without doing. Human *being*. Being more open, relaxed, aware, compassionate, and generous, with less trying and scurrying about, exerting our wills and egos at each other and the environment. Being satisfied with "enough." Knowing when we have enough. Being present in the here-and-now—this very moment—with awareness and acceptance of what *is*. This is not something we get much practice at or praise for in our present culture.

Greed—the incessant hunger for more, as if it were possible to escape the underlying insecurity of life by surrounding ourselves with material possessions.

Fear—that we're somehow lacking as individuals, that we don't have control of life, that we're going to die.

These base instincts drive unconscious consumption. And advertisers pitch their messages to reach into our unconscious and stir them up. *This* or *that* product will keep us young, enhance our power, make us more popular, or provide the sense of safety that we seek.

What's really needed is an evolution of consciousness, an advancement of moral and emotional maturity, clear-seeing awareness of the realities of life— and our life in particular—along with the courage to simply recognize these old emotions (fear and greed) as part of the human repertoire of experience without unawarely acting on them. It's possible to simply notice when fear or greed arise—"Oh, there's that impulse for *more* again"—and then be conscious in the present moment of whether to consider it a mandate for action or not. This momentary pause with awareness between the impulse and the corresponding action is what allows us to break the unconscious addictive habit. We become conscious of the impulse without acting on it. In that moment, we have an opportunity to examine it a little more closely—"Hmmm. This feels weird. What is this *really* about?" We bring awareness into the moment. Consciousness grows, unconsciousness wanes, eventually a new habit of examining our impulses, rather than automatically acting them out, is born. This is how consciousness evolves. This is the development of the skillful means necessary to move forward as a species without overshooting the carrying capacity of our environment.

This process can allow us to have the full range of human emotional experience, but choose consciously which feelings to act on and which to simply experience without acting on. Such restraint elevates us above our base instincts and makes possible the emergence of a global community based on higher sentiments than greed and fear. It clears a path toward compassion and generosity and looking beyond one's own reference groups and historical time, above and beyond the illusion of separation, toward a truly integrated, interdependent, sustainable global community. Because that's what we are, whether we like it or not, whether we recognize it nor not. We are a part of the web of life, and fear and greed simply don't serve us well, as a species, anymore. In fact, continuing to unconsciously act aggressively toward each other could actually lead to our ultimate demise. It's time for humanity to grow up to the next stage of development, take an evolutionary leap forward, learn to share, and be nice to each other. It's time to hold hands and look both ways.

PART ONE: WHY THE BOOK?

The Current Cultural Momentum is Changeable, But...

THE CURRENT CULTURAL MOMENTUM IS CHANGEABLE, BUT ... IT'S NOT EASY. It's hard to swim against the tide of consumerism and corporate mass-media indoctrination. It's not easy to live a life that is congruent with values of eco-logical sustainability and social equality in an economic system that strives for on-demand fulfillment of our every desire and is so demanding of our time at every turn. For those making efforts to birth the emerging culture, it can be difficult to know what to order at a restaurant where there are no local-seasonal-organic choices, or what "holiday gifts" to get for people you genuinely love and respect, but who hold totally different values than your own. And how does one get around town in five different directions in a single day, to take care of all those nagging errands that need doing, without resorting to the use of a car? The way this culture is set up, it's not easy to live congruently with progressive, sustainable values. It can also be very awkward and discouraging to find yourself attempting to communicate what seem like obvious, valid concerns, across a divide, to someone you thought you knew well, and really care about, only to run into a brick wall—"I don't want to hear that." Or—"Man, you're just full of rosy optimism aren't you?"

So yes, the current cultural momentum is changeable, but ... it's not easy. It requires addressing change on multiple levels. There is plenty of work to do on all fronts. For example, Joanna Macy[1] suggests that some of the work will involve "stopping actions" that slow the damage being done—like stopping the clear-cutting of forests, or halting the dumping of persistent pollutants into watersheds. For others, the work will involve deconstructing and trans-forming societal institutions that no longer serve the common good, but rather the economic interests of an elite few. And for yet others, the work will be to spread a shift in consciousness—an awakening to the realization of our interconnectedness, as a species, with each other and the web of life all around us.

Yes, the currently unsustainable, unsatisfying, media-conditioned, fear-and-greed-based cultural momentum is changeable, but … it will take effort. It will also take courage, a willingness to stand on our own two feet, unsupported at times, presenting an unpopular view, in the face of external resistance. In addition, the magnitude of cultural adaptation we are talking about will require perseverance over time, the application of skillful means, and a supportive community of like-minded individuals offering restorative connection for those making the effort to transform societies' institutions. While we may very well have to stand alone in some situations, it's important to remember that *we don't have to do everything alone all the time.* Close, solid, social support can make the work easier, more effective, and more fun.

My personal journey has led me through rage, fear, and grief about the state of affairs we find ourselves in. I have shifted, internally and externally, from fighting against, or trying to fix what is broken, to leaning in the direction I would like to see things progress. I favor a vision of an emerging culture, a global community that is healthier, more cooperative, more compassionate, more stable, sustainable and fulfilling than our current arrangement. This means putting my energy increasingly "forward" to those sprouting ideas and initiatives that seem to be leading the way to a future in which I am interested in living. I believe that by cultivating a consciousness of FOR words we are more likely to create the world we want, than by swirling in anger and upset about what we *don't* want. Atlee[2] reminds us that "being against something does not build that which is needed."

I'm generally not a big proponent of Coue's method or simplistic "positive thinking" as a way to navigate one's life. I've read too much Freud. But it does sometimes seem that what we fill our consciousness with has an affect on the possibilities we see, and the circumstances we create in our lives—individually and collectively. Funny how that works.

---

[1] Macy, J., and Brown, M.Y. (1998).

[2] Atlee, T., and Zubizarreta, R. (2003).

EXAMPLES OF "FOR" WORDS THAT I FIND ENCOURAGING AT THIS JUNCTURE INCLUDE:

Active, Acknowledge, Adapt, Alert, Alliance, Allow, Alternative, Appreciation, Appropriate Technology, Arising, Authentic, Awareness, Balance, Beauty, Biosphere, Biology, Blooming, Breakthrough, Breathe (yes, you—right now), Caring, Carrying Capacity, Charity, Choice, Collective, Collective Intelligence, Compassion, Compliment, Community, Confederation, Conscious, Conscious Evolution, Conscience, Collaboration, Cooperation, Cooperative, Courage, Creativity, Critical Thinking, Decentralized, Democracy, Dialogue, Discussion, Diversity, Eco, Ecology, Education, Equal, Equitable, Emergent, Emerging, Enough, Environment, Evolution, Evolutionary, Fair, Fair Trade, Faith, Feedback, Feeling, Freedom, Free Speech, Fulfilling, Future Generations, Generosity, Gifting, Giving, Global, Global Community, (The) Great Turning, Green, Growing, H2, Hydrogen, Healing, Health, (the) Highest Truth, Holistic, Hope, Human, Humanity, Human Spirit, Inclusive, Indigenous, Intelligence, Innovative, Instant Runoff Voting, Institutional Analysis, Interconnected, Interdependent, Interrelated, Inquiry, Justice, Learning, Liberty, Life-Enhancing, Life-Positive, Life-Supporting, Living Systems, Local, Long-Term, Long-Term Goals, Long-Term Vision, Like, Love, Meaningful, Moderation, Moral Maturity, Nature, Natural, Network, Networking, Social Networking, Noble, Noble Deeds, Noble Intentions, Noticing, Open, Opportunity, Organic, Paradigm, Paradigm Shift, Participatory, Peace, Perceptive, Permaculture, Personal Growth, Power-With, Pristine, Progressive, Pro-Social, Pro-Choice, Pro-Justice, Questions, Reach, Renewable, Renewable Energy, Resource, Resources, Renewable Resources, Resourceful, Respect, Responsibility, Personal Responsibility, Collective Responsibility, Revolution, Revolutionary, (R)evolutionary, Self-Awareness, Self-Determination, Self-Esteem, Sensitivity, Sensing, Seven Generations, Sharing, Simple, Simple Pleasures, Simple Living, Simplicity, Voluntary Simplicity, Social Evolution, Soil, Solar Power, Stand, Stand For, Stand Up, Stand Up For, (take a) Stand, Stretch, Support, Synergy, System, Systems Theory, Whole Systems, Supportive, Sustainable, Thriving, Thinking, Tilth, Trans-National Peoples Alliance, Trust, Vegan, Vegetarian, Vision, Voluntary, Watershed, Web of Life, Welfare, Whole, Wholesome, Wind Power, Wisdom, Wishing, Worthwhile, Yes. YES!

Personal Growth, Moral Maturity, Social Evolution, and Human Potential

FROM THE MOMENT OF CONCEPTION, HUMAN DEVELOPMENT IS UNDERWAY. Numerous different-yet-integrated aspects of our "self" begin unfolding along their separate-yet-interconnected paths, each with its own unique set of stages, functions, and potentials. The overall general progression of evolution and of the self in particular seems to be from simpler, homogenous, and less capable toward more complex, differentiated, and sophisticated functioning. Simultaneously, at varying rates, and to varying degrees—depending on how completely we realize our full human potential in any given area at any given moment—each line of development proceeds toward its greatest capacity, shaped by the combination of our inherited DNA, the circumstantial forces surrounding us (parents, society, the biological environment in which we live), and the choices/intentions/behaviors we generate and exert on our surroundings as individuals manifesting some measure of self-determination in life. Individually and together these factors either encourage or discourage the unfolding process of moving toward our greatest potential.

Each line of development—physiological, cognitive, emotional, social, moral, sexual, spiritual, and so forth, has an effect on our experience and our functioning. Each is important. Not all are developed to the same degree at any given point. The experience of "personal growth" is often one of discovering that a particular aspect of our self has been lagging in its development. It's as though we grow a new capacity to feel, think, perceive, or experience some aspect of life that has been missing. We feel more "deeply", come to understand our self and life from a "broader" perspective, feel that we have finally reached a "higher" stage of development. It feels great—like we finally understand that irksome *something* that has kept us stuck in a narrow, repetitive, frustrating life. Something that we've been tripping over in the dark is now illuminated so that we can see and walk around it rather than continuing to stumble over it—"Aha! Yes, now I see."

When these moments occur, it seems as if we finally have life figured out and know how we must live from this day forth. Yet the question remains whether this process of expanding awareness and self-understanding *is ever really finished*. Is it possible for any human being to fully understand everything about themselves and life? Or is human potential truly limitless? How big *is* consciousness? What *are* the bounds of awareness?

These questions are best debated by philosophers, and have been for ages. They also have some relevance to our discussion of social evolution and sustainability. And while endless distinctions can be made (and careers built upon) the differences between various developmental schema, the purpose of this book is to focus on those conceptualizations that are useful for our goal of learning to communicate more effectively about the challenging circumstances we find ourselves in at this juncture as a society. The goal is to find a way to successfully and collectively steer our course toward a more sustainable, just and fulfilling global community. To reiterate, we are trying to understand why it is that some people seem to understand the larger ecological context of humanity, and how the degradation of the environment diminishes the health, well-being, and prospects of civilization, while others do not. We are trying to understand how to best communicate across this divide in our everyday lives with people we genuinely care about.

By focusing our discussion through *that* lens, we can learn much that is useful from those who have outlined various paths of human development. With a nod to political correctness, it must be noted that there are reasonable arguments from those who object to notions of development that include "levels" or "stages" that imply "higher" and "lower" development, and "more" or "less" advanced. But such arguments are largely aimed at the ways in which hierarchies have been used as tools of oppression in the service of empire. Most people understand and accept, consciously as well as intuitively, that the life of a human infant is more "valuable" than the life of a malaria-carrying mosquito that might infect the infant. Thus a hierarchy of life forms is acknowledged. Some *beings* (sentient life forms) simply seem to be more "evolved" and are therefore more valued—for their complexity, their level of awareness, their potential, and so forth. This is, indeed, a slippery area, for one does not want to put down or minimize the value of any sentient being to the *whole*. But this notion of levels is one which this author will assume can be accepted on a practical level, without digression into endless philosophical debate and consternation, for the purposes outlined above.

Just as social evolution has taken humanity from bands of hunter-gatherers through an era of settled, agriculturally based villages and guild-craft towns, to industrial cities that now utilize an information-based, global economic system that ravages the environment, some would say that we are in need of a *next* evolutionary step in our journey as a species. Many are awakening to a higher awareness of our interconnectedness with each other and with all other species—the "web of life"—living at *this* historical moment within a finite, fragile biosphere. This dawning awareness generally, but not necessarily, requires that more fundamental needs (food, security, etc.) are being met on a regular basis. In this regard, those who live in relative peace and prosperity have a greater moral responsibility to lead the way forward in a manner that encompasses the needs of those who have less.

Consciously taking this next evolutionary step forward requires a fairly strong, healthy, well-functioning psychological ego. It also requires some recognition that one's greater sense of Self somehow, sometimes, goes beyond this smaller psychological self which is, after all, primarily just a constellation of thoughts and self-images based on identification with various ego/personality traits, memories, and so forth. This realization of a larger Self is sometimes described as a shift in the locus of "I," a shift in identification of the "self" from the smaller, individual point of view (ego), to a larger, contextual awareness within which one's individual life, personality, and development is continuously unfolding.

From this larger perspective, this contextual locus of "I," many (but not necessarily all) unsustainable behaviors and attitudes dissolve and drift away without effort. It becomes clear that trying to solidify and fortify a particular set of mental constructs is not only pointless, but self-defeating—both individually and collectively. Realizing this makes a lot of other things easier, too. Emotional growth unfolds with much less drama when resistance to one's feelings is lessened. There is an increased ability to tolerate frustration, inconvenience, discomfort, and so forth, without "acting out" in self-defeating and environmentally destructive ways. The abilities to wait (patience), to care and to share expand naturally without feeling put upon. Moral maturity progresses from egocentric through various stages of ever-expanding personal reference groups (family, community, region, nation) toward an awareness of our interdependence as a global community with limited resources. It dawns on us that we are actually just one part of an interconnected, complex web of life that we don't really understand very well yet. Certainly not well enough to be driving over it with bulldozers.

So individually, and collectively, manifesting in numerous different aspects, at varying rates, through different levels and stages, it would appear that we (and all of "life" of which we are a part) are progressing along an evolutionary journey toward ... this is the Great Mystery. Let us have some humility in relation to this upward-reaching, creative life force that temporarily animates us as a single point of view for a relatively short time span, and recognize that what we share with *all* living beings is that we are *alive*. We are *all* expressions of the same indefinable life force evolving toward ever-greater levels of complexity and integration.

An increasing and accelerating number of people are beginning to awaken to this consciousness of interconnectedness. Many are beginning to see the potential benefits of marveling in this awareness rather than killing each other over whose limited conceptual system about it is right. This is the evolutionary step forward that will allow us to coexist as a global species in a sustainable manner with material sufficiency, greater equality, maximal health, and well-being. It is the path of moral maturity, generosity, and compassion which leads toward our highest potential.

Part One

Why The Book?

The current cultural momentum is:

- unsustainable
- unsatisfying
- conditioned
- fear and greed based
- changeable, but...

Personal Growth
Moral Maturity
Social Evolution
Human Potential

Part Two

Three Things

Understand the person you are talking with:

- **Section One**
  their unique
  CHARACTER STYLE

- **Section Two**
  their
  CURRENT WORLDVIEW

- **Section Three**
  which
  EXISTENTIAL CONCERN
  they are struggling with

Part Three

Techniques

You might try:

- listening
- "between the lines"
- parallel their arguments
- question assumptions
- change the context
- stick to common ground
- applaud all steps
- other ideas...

Part Four

Examples

Imagine yourself in:

- An Awkward Event
- A Workplace Conflict
- Air Travel Delay

PART TWO

Three Things To Know About Those Who Don't Seem To Understand That "THE HOUSE IS ON FIRE!"

Introduction: Three Things to Know

AS STATED EARLIER, THREE THINGS WE NEED TO UNDERSTAND AND KEEP IN mind about the people we are talking with are: 1) their individual psychological character style and its unique constellation of ego defenses; 2) their current worldview which offers some clues about what resonates with them as true, plausible, and appealing, as well as what turns them off or makes them discount your message before really considering it; and 3) which existential concern has been aroused in them by their consideration of where humanity appears to be headed.

Understanding these three things enables us to devise a communication strategy that: 1) gets past (through) their conditioned defensive layer without snagging; 2) appeals to their current view of how the world works (with an implicit invitation to consider expanding that view to include a little more of yours); and 3) soothes any existential angst stirred up by the bad news you present.

We will begin this section by looking briefly at how character is formed, and the purpose it serves in our attempts to adapt to the vicissitudes of life. This will be followed by a series of brief descriptive portraits of various character types as we know them in daily life.

Next, we will make a distinction between a person's individual character style and their current worldview. While both exert an influence on perception and behavioral choices, and there is often some degree of overlap between the two, there isn't necessarily a direct correlation. Understanding and respecting the distinction can be important for effective communication.

Finally, we will take a sober look at those ever-unpopular sources of existential suffering with which we all must cope: death, uncertainty, meaninglessness, and aloneness. These givens of existence lie in the background of our lives (or beneath the surface, to be more psychoanalytic about it), exerting an unceasing influence on our interactions and stance in life. Operating outside of awareness, they often contribute to communication difficulties as their arousal requires heightened defense by the threatened and embattled ego. Bringing awareness to this dynamic can help soften the blows of reality that we offer across the divide by putting us in touch with a deeper sense of humanity, humility, compassion, and spirit—increasing our sense of connectedness as human beings.

Part One

Why The Book?

The current cultural momentum is:

- unsustainable
- unsatisfying
- conditioned
- fear and greed based
- changeable, but...

- Personal Growth
- Moral Maturity
- Social Evolution
- Human Potential

Part Two

Three Things

Understand the person you are talking with:

- **Section One**
  their unique
  CHARACTER STYLE

- **Section Two**
  their
  CURRENT WORLDVIEW

- **Section Three**
  which
  EXISTENTIAL CONCERN
  they are struggling with

Part Three

Techniques

You might try:

- listening
- "between the lines"
- parallel their arguments
- question assumptions
- change the context
- stick to common ground
- applaud all steps
- other ideas...

Part Four

Examples

Imagine yourself in:

- An Awkward Event

- A Workplace Conflict

- Air Travel Delay

Section 1) Character Style

ONE WAY OF ATTEMPTING TO UNDERSTAND HUMAN BEHAVIOR IS FROM THE perspective of need gratification. We all have needs, lots of needs. We have basic physiological needs, emotional needs, social needs, spiritual needs, and so forth. When, as a living organism, we are motivated by these needs to go out into our surrounding biological and social environment, our needs are met or not, to a greater or lesser degree, by our success at finding what we need. Pleasure and pain are the base indicators of how well we are doing at getting our needs met at any given moment. When a need is satisfied, we experience pleasure. Unmet needs are experienced as displeasure or pain. Pleasure and pain are commonly known by their accompanying affects—the more nuanced "feelings" along four basic experiential spectrums—joy, sadness, anger, or fear—to which all other feelings tend to resolve upon analysis.

The intensity of a feeling—the degree of its energetic charge—is also something that must be taken into consideration. Both positive and negative emotions can be experienced at times as too intense, and therefore must be modulated and defended against. This is one role of a well-functioning ego —to avoid overwhelm. Individuals differ in their capacity to tolerate intense emotions. Consider, for example, the life of a "thrill seeker" versus those who are unreceptive to excitation in their lives. We all have our personal thresholds where intensity becomes problematic; it is at this juncture that the notion of "defense" comes into play. We all have our ways of defending against experiences which are too intense for us, ways in which we deny, suppress, avoid, project, compensate, and "squirm" in our attempts to escape the intensity of a feeling. In psychoanalytic jargon we refer to these maneuvers as ego defense mechanisms.

Behavioral conditioning results, over time, from successfully avoiding pain and finding pleasure. Our strategy solidifies as we find ourselves relying on our most successful coping mechanisms. Thus we adapt to our environment. The characteristic ways that we cope with our lives become known as our character or personality. At some level, we are known by the unique constellation of characterological defenses that we have come to rely on as the most effective in navigating our lives through the environment(s) in which we find ourselves. Nature has set the limits within which nurture has shaped our way of being in the world.

In a nutshell, needs take us out into the world and result in pleasure or pain. Pleasure or pain lead to the myriad shadings, layerings, and combinations of the four basic affects: joy, sadness, anger, fear. When these feelings are too intense, too troublesome or disruptive, too displeasurable, we (mostly unconsciously) employ a variety of defense mechanisms which reduce the intensity, enhancing our ability to cope with whatever situation we find ourselves in. Over time, the successful defenses become behaviorally conditioned into our characterological "strategy" for moving through life. Thus our unique character or personality by which others know us comes into being. This predictable, characteristic set of behaviors, attitudes, mannerisms, and so forth, is one of the Three Things to understand about the person with whom you are communicating. It affects their ability to hear and respond to you agreeably.

Character Style: Common Constellations

WE ARE ALL UNIQUE INDIVIDUALS. AND OBVIOUSLY, THERE IS MORE TO people than the limited glimpses we come to know as their predictable behavior. All of us are capable of change and are, in fact, ever-changing and *becoming*. That being said, there are also a number of commonly recogniz-able character types. Sometimes called our "personality"[1] or "neurotic style,"[2] these identifiable patterns of adaptation tend to be fairly consistent strategies of characterological defense.

It's important to not get stuck in thinking that a person is *this* or *that* "type," because we all manifest aspects of *all* of the various character strategies. We are *all* mixes, with more and less emphasis on various types, in an endless array of unique blends. *That's what makes us all so different.* That we all share some measure of every style is our basis for empathy, as well—we can relate! We know how others suffer, because we too suffer in similar (if less or more prominent) ways within our own unique blend of defensive patterns. It's useful to try to think of these constellations of defensive maneuvers not so much as rigid, distinct types, but more as preferred styles of adaptation to life that have worked the best for an individual over time. Patterns of adaptation are not to be confused with the ever-changing individual temporarily using them. Every person, every style, every type has its own gifts and limitations. All are important and to be valued for the unique contribution to the *whole* that they are capable of making.

It's also important to recognize that characterological armor becomes stronger (defends more vigorously) when under attack. So, in general, pushing and being "right" (that they are "wrong") will only lock you into a power struggle that you are likely to lose. We are all masters at winning on our own turf—having spent a lifetime practicing that particular strategy.

The value in recognizing the predominant character style of the person we are talking with is that it offers some understanding of the characteristic ways in which they will be likely to defend against unpleasant feelings. This understanding enables us to tailor our communications so as to *not* arouse further, stronger, more rigid defense on their part. Doing this tends to foster both an increase of pleasure during the interaction and an increased likelihood of truly hearing each other's thinking without distortion. This, of course, is the goal: to get past their defenses to where consideration of new information can result in expanded awareness and, ultimately, behavior change.

There is an assumption being made here: that if a rational person of average intelligence can drop their guard and genuinely consider the possible urgency of the various challenges we face as a civilization, they will naturally feel an inherent motivation to take reasonable action in order to prevent detrimental circumstances from occurring. We shall see. Here, then, is a brief introduction to a number of different character types.

---

[1] DSM-IV-TR. (2000).

[2] Shapiro, D. (1965, 1981).

Self-Important

When Self-Confidence becomes Selfishness

A healthy self-esteem is generally considered a good thing. People with "low" self-esteem suffer, subjectively, from lives filled with feelings of unworthiness, moving head-down along the outskirts of life. People with "high" self-esteem, by contrast, often rise to positions of leadership. They stand out in a crowd as self-assured. They know what they want, and they usually get it. They tend to be extroverted by nature and cultivate a charismatic air that attracts followers who are motivated to follow their lead.

When confronted with "inconvenient truths" about the environment and prospects for social and economic progress, these individuals instinctively (characteristically) reject the notion that it could ever affect them personally. They have such confidence in themselves, their abilities, their specialness, that they genuinely feel that they are above and beyond the reach of such tragic, but mundane, concerns. Unless, of course, the current popular trend —sustainability—can be used to aggrandize more ego-inflating attention. Politically savvy, they may "rise to the occasion" if it garners them more status. This might be useful information for eliciting their help in redirect-ing the course of civilization. You might be able to make a direct, flattering appeal to their "unique special reason for existence on the planet at this momentous time in history."

Individuals with a predominance of this character style generally expect to be treated as special by others and are unashamed about their ambitions and talents. When successful, it is generally because they do, indeed, have talents which are admirable. Those who are less successful often lack the real talent to back their strutting and look pitifully desperate as they resort to shrewd selfishness and petty displays of arrogance in an attempt to maintain a failing self-esteem.

When taken to an extreme, self-importance becomes what we commonly refer to as narcissism. It's important to recognize that there are different types of narcissism. Psychoanalytic literature defines in great detail the role and aspects of healthy narcissism. The narcissism we are concerned with in this discussion is that by which an individual's healthy self-esteem has become annoyingly self-centered, self-absorbed, and self-defeating. Such individuals can be demanding, manipulative, and very "trying" to be around. But even within this latter category of narcissism, there appear to be two sub-types: a "deprivation-based" narcissism (didn't get enough maternal nurturing early on) and an "indulgence-based" narcissism (got their way more often than was good for them). It's important to understand which type of narcissistic defense pattern you are talking to, because while both will, on the surface, display similar interpersonal characteristics, beneath the surface, one (deprivation-based) is really needing a warm, nurturing, reflective response from you, while the other (indulgence-based) is actually needing—not wanting, but needing—frustration of their arrogant stance in order to mature emotionally (and thereby accept that, perhaps, global climate change *might* affect them after all). A notable sense of collapsing bravado (a faltering of the false self) and depressive affect will typically accompany the arrival of any realization that dethrones them. This can be understood as a validation that you have succeeded in getting through the layers of narcissistic defense to the more authentic human underneath. They have just had a meaningful, if disturbing, glimpse of reality. This is the time to switch to a more compassionate stance, empathizing with their suffering, so that they feel accepted by you even though they are not as great as they tried to lead you to believe. This makes it safe for them to consider more deeply the contradictory information, integrate the insights, and manifest changes in their life accordingly —such as becoming a "star" for sustainability—a good role for them in the Great Turning.

Suspicious

When Alert becomes Paranoid

Those whose environments required them to be alert in order to avoid unpleasantness typically develop into highly perceptive individuals. These individuals are often well aware of how things add up and are quick to notice incongruities between what people say and what they do. Not much escapes their notice. Even the slightest incongruities are picked up by their exceptional radar and monitored for further indications of a possible threat. Such individuals can make strange bedfellows for environmentalists. They often share concerns about environmental degradation, but are much more likely to dig in with "guns and gold" as isolated survivalists, than to seek community consensus on how to proceed. Healthy vigilance can quickly turn into paranoid withdrawal and projection of ill-intent onto others, where what they feel like doing to others is misperceived as others scheming to do to them.

They are survivors. They are well prepared for the eventualities of a dangerous downturn. By continually scanning their environment for anything that is not right, they feel less likely to be caught off guard—"Just because you're paranoid doesn't mean they aren't out to get you."

When talking with these individuals, you need to stay aware that arousing their anxiety will make them dig in deeper and mistrust you. They will be exquisitely aware of any mixed messages coming from you, or any hidden motivations in you, even those that may lie outside your own awareness. The most subtle distortions of the truth will be taken as betrayal and serve as grounds for retaliation, sooner or later. It's not that they are incapable of friendship, but they are cautious, slow to warm up, and easily repelled by the appearance of disloyalty.

Such individuals often find their niche within the environmental movement as social critics who are not afraid to confront abuses of power with devastating accuracy. You definitely want them on your side—not against you—although their propensity for pointing out incongruities can be annoying even within their own camp.

At its less sociable extreme, such a stance in life becomes what we commonly refer to as paranoid. This phrase is sometimes bantered around in light-hearted accusations among friends, but in its clinical definition, it is hardly a joke. Such individuals truly struggle with pervasive apprehension. They are consumed with mistrust and are convinced that others are out to humiliate them. They can be argumentative and uncompromising in a self-defeating way. They seem to create the mistreatment they expect from others, and are particularly uncomfortable around people of higher rank. Projection is their basic defensive strategy—it is not they who are wrong, weak, or harbor ill intent. These mental contents are projected onto others in an attempt to protect their own fragile self-esteem—the underlying fear that they *are* wrong, bad, weak, helpless, and wishing harm on others. They project these unacceptable feelings outward and then see them (and attack them) in others and the untrustworthy world.

They are very tender underneath and easily hurt by what they perceive as criticism, so you must proceed slowly and back off if you feel yourself locking horns with them, or see them pulling away into a defensive stance. If you persist, they will only become more hostile, defensive, and secretive. You don't want to rigidify their stance. It will only result in their becoming more suspicious of you and more black-and-white in their thinking. Give them some room and some warmth and they will be more likely to respond by considering the possibility that they overlooked something of value in your argument. Don't crowd them or expose their thinking as "wrong" (i.e., don't humiliate them). Give them steady reassurance that they are safe and can retreat any time they need to. If they feel safe and accepted rather than trapped, they can be among the most articulate observers of unsustainable behavior in your community. Go slowly.

Organized and Efficient

When Conscientious becomes Compulsive

For individuals with a predominance of this character strategy, life is just one large spreadsheet, or so they wish. These hard-working, achievement-oriented individuals like a clearly laid-out approach to life. They like to have it all under control, be "mapped out" on which way they are heading, and know what comes next. They've thought everything through and have a plan—in meticulous detail. They're organized, efficient, and disciplined about pursuing their goals. Don't we all wish we had it "together" like this? Well, maybe not. Their strength at focused determination can, under pressure (internal as much as external), become a burdensome workaholic lifestyle with little actual fulfillment. They often have difficulty letting down and relaxing. They are driven by "shoulds" and a fear of disapproval. Upon completion of a task, they cannot seem to enjoy the moment, even for a moment. Instead, they push on and persevere with their endless to-do list, hoping to one day be good enough (i.e., perfect) in the eyes of others. This makes them, of course, a real asset to any organization (e.g., an environmental non-profit agency) because of their ability to keep track of the details and plow through the work. Just don't mess up the papers on their desk, or go digging through their drawers without an invitation. If you frustrate their perfectionist tendencies, they can be quick to anger.

This character type has been very valuable to the global industrial-growth economy in its relentless exploitation of natural resources. They make good, conventional corporate drones and bureaucrats. They genuinely want to do the right thing and often have strong opinions about what that *is*. This character style is an easy fit with the traditional pop-culture, neo-liberal economic philosophy. And they generally have the justifications and rationalizations at hand to support their convictions. Challenging their stance only strengthens their defense. Direct opposition is a futile exercise; it only energizes their dogged determination to win. And win they must. They can't stand, and will never admit to, being "wrong." It's far too humiliating. To avoid a power struggle that you can never win—they are consummate arguers and will wear you down with hair-splitting details—try just listening and letting them run out their argument. Then, having grasped the essence of their point, try saying something like, "I hear you, I understand where you're coming from."

This style's tendency toward stubborn "rightness" is one reason why getting them on the side of sane environmental policies and social change efforts is so important. They can easily understand concepts like "externalized costs" and "depletion of non-renewable resources." These ideas make sense to them. They are thrifty by nature, so notions like conservation and recycling are congruent with their approach to life and will resonate as correct. Acknowledge this and applaud (reinforce) their steps toward reduced consumerism as rational, given the current state of diminishing resources. Recognize that the content of their focus can broaden (slowly) to include reasonable new information, especially if it is well documented. They are good people. We all are—regardless of the adaptive patterns we currently rely on.

Hot and Cold

When Warm and Fun becomes "Whoa, what just happened?"

The first time you meet one of these individuals it feels like they've been your best friend forever. There's an unmistakable instant rapport, a strong connection. You go home feeling really good about the interaction, thinking how special they are, and look forward to seeing them again soon. They, also, have the experience of having just found their new best friend. The speed and depth with which your lives become entangled can be truly amazing. And then, characteristically, something happens. Most likely you haven't got a clue what. But you find yourself on the receiving end of a major upset. The intensity and primitiveness of their emotional upheaval makes you take a step back—"Whoa. What just happened? Did I say or do something?" Your stepping back to gain some distance for perspective only seems to exacerbate the situation. It's perceived and experienced by them as abandonment. Suddenly you find yourself out of their life spinning in a circle wondering if maybe you didn't get too close too fast. This is the story of their lives—a roller coaster of relationships. They drop in and out of love, jobs, and locations with breathtaking speed, leaving a trail of bedraggled ex-best friends and lovers.

Hot and cold. At first people or situations are all good, on a pedestal, it's destiny that you've met. Then, after a while, you find yourself becoming a little tired of their constant need for engagement. You want a little space, some distance from their incessant need to be involved in your every thought and feeling. And that does it. Like a flip-switch, in their mind, you go from being the one who is cherished and needed, to being all bad, extremely evil, a horrid individual. They dump their rage on you—actually if feels like "into" you—and they storm out of your life.

Individuals struggling under the weight of this particular adaptive strategy tend to jump into each new situation, each new relationship, with both feet and little regard for personal boundaries—their own or the other person's. They seek a deep emotional and physical connection in every moment. And it is this need for such intense engagement that exhausts most people relatively quickly. Their "urge to merge" (possess and be possessed) sets others back on their heels gasping for air. But bringing up your need to "take some space" only triggers their sensitivity to "abandonment" and sets off an enormous, irrational, accusatory demand for more closeness. Like squeezing a wet bar of soap in one's hand, the stronger they try to grasp hold, the more distance others seem to need. They come up empty-handed over and over again. They are so intensely "needy" that they drive people away with their inability to be separate and feel whole on their own. This causes them to miss out on the intimacy they so desperately desire. They cannot exist, they fear, without being attached. And if you prove to be untrustworthy as someone they can attach to (merge with), they quickly move on to the next person or situation. Thus, their emotional life, their interpersonal life, their work life can best be characterized as stormy and fast-moving.

They are likely to be drawn to the community aspect of progressive social and environmental groups. The notions of global community and group consensus give them a place to feel connected, and therefore safe—merged into the mass. Their tendency for passionate emotional experience makes the more successful among them good at artistic expressions which grab audiences with their raw intensity. In this capacity they can make a welcome contribution to marketing efforts for sustainability. But you definitely want to keep them out of the PR department of your organization, as they will tend to create damaging drama with those you seek to impress. They have trouble casually "schmoozing," since every little comment is imbued with great meaning. They don't take anything lightly. And, because they are so emotionally reactive, they tend to not be good negotiators. They put their *all* into whatever they are doing and could not hold a "poker-face" to save their own life.

However, because they can be so engaging, "high energy," and spontaneous, they can be really fun to be around. This is why you fall in love with them the minute you meet them. They inspire others with their enthusiasm. But their ability to follow through with consistent effort over the long term is not a good position of responsibility for them. Inviting them to be door greeters at an environmental conference would be a good job for them. Everyone would feel genuinely welcomed with sincere warmth. Just make sure they're not going home after the conference with your most important donor.

Flamboyant

When Good Taste becomes a Shallow Show

Individuals with a predominance of this character style are the life of the party. In fact, where they are is where the party *is*—in a good way. They carry their extroverted aliveness *with them* into every situation. They are fun and exciting to be around, entertaining to watch, and make a lavish display of warmth and caring toward others which most people enjoy. They take special care to look nice and value aesthetic beauty in their lives. They seem to always know just the right thing to say to make people around them feel good. Being "on stage" is where they live. They can swoop into a room full of dull, joyless people and have it swirling with upbeat enthusiasm in an instant—often just with their dramatic entrance. They are great storytellers and can turn the most mundane explanation of where they've just been into a theatrical performance—although the details might be a little distorted to add emotional impact.

Those whose conditioning has led to relying on this particular strategy tend to be physically affectionate, emotionally expressive, and have colorful imaginations. Their presentation is fashionable and has a keen sense of style. They know what's hip this season and are usually wearing it. They intuit what is "catchy" and what will resonate with a pop-culture audience. This makes it easy for them to come up with good advertising slogans, poster images, and so forth. But their creativity can sometimes be a little thin, lacking the depth that is generally a requisite of "great" art. Their focus is often more on drawing attention to themselves than reaching for authentic deep expression.

They are not known for being deep thinkers. They are "feelers" and like to be the center of attention. When all eyes are on them, they really shine. This can sometimes result in their becoming a little too naïve and trusting of others. Flattery endears them. And their hunger for more can result in their becoming too quickly involved in romantic relationships and melodrama. They love intrigue, gossip, and soap operas. But their seductive charm can get them into trouble—especially with those who know how to manipulate such individuals. They tend to have a hard time tolerating boredom and are generally not good with details, routines, and finances. An offer to escape (drop everything and run off) into an exciting, romantic fantasy weekend with a new lover can sometimes leave them involved in situations in which they are taken advantage of.

When this character type is viewed from the more dysfunctional end of the spectrum, it becomes evident that these individuals struggle with an unsettled sense of self. They can be restless and can require lots of adoration from others to maintain their self-esteem. They might have trouble *not* acting on their impulses to escape intolerable impatience. Low frustration tolerance can make it difficult to resist indulging in immediate gratification. Shopping sprees ("retail therapy") can result in credit card disasters. Long-range planning and sticking to a budget fly out the window when their self-control falters. When confronted, they may become highly emotional—yelling, crying, stomping around. On the good side, they don't hold a grudge and are easily persuaded out of a child-like tantrum with a few compliments and offers of indulgence (i.e., caving in to their demands)—as long as it happens right *now*.

At the furthest end of this spectrum, those with this character style can become quite desperate. Individuals whose functioning is distorted by the extreme version of this adaptive pattern can resort to dramatic and provocative attempts to draw attention to themselves. They feel utterly empty and horrid inside without constant praise. It's important to *not* overreact if/when they do this. Reassure them that they are appreciated, but remain firm about your requirements. Don't engage in their emotionality—you'll never win. Thankfully, this extreme version represents very few individuals.

The more common, less-extreme version of this character type is much more likely to cross paths with you in your daily life. As noted above, these more moderately scripted individuals can be very entertaining and charismatic. Their extroversion can be useful to your organization, particularly in an "on-stage" role. Public speaking or presentations for progressive change is a function where they can really shine and tell a good story; they love the "all eyes on me" attention. It's a good role for them in the Great Turning that we are undertaking as a civilization.

Moping

When Serious becomes Sad and Listless

It's hard to not be depressed about what's going on in the world. "If you're not outraged, you're not paying attention" says the bumper sticker. Individuals with this character type *are* paying attention. They're taking a hard look at what's going on and they're not happy about what they see. In fact, an argument can be made that people who feel discouraged about the current state of the world actually see reality more clearly (and deeply) than more light-hearted others. While others are channel-surfing past the news in search of entertainment and escape, these sober individuals feel (but don't easily express) the tragedy of it all. Some would argue that they focus too much on the negative. Individuals with a predominance of this character strategy would dismiss those critics as naïve and shallow.

We live in a culture that distracts us at every turn and promotes denial and "positive thinking," a culture that promises consumer bliss. But these folks don't buy it. Individuals with this type of conditioning are not as caught up in the illusion. They don't really care about going along with the crowd or being popular. They're too sharp for that. They're keeping an eye on what's *really* going on. And what's *really* going on is *not* something to be happy about. They size others and situations up accurately and can offer a useful (if painfully accurate) appraisal at any time. So stop enjoying your smiley-face lives already. Things are not great. The glass is only half full, and many have empty glasses. Why is *this* a reason to rejoice?

Sound like anybody you know? Probably. Most of us, at times, can relate to such feelings. Yet we manage to find ways to balance the seriousness of life with what reasonable pleasures life has to offer. Most of us would probably turn out to be wimps if life ever required us to endure such truly harsh circumstances as many people in world face today. These individuals would likely be able to show us how to carry our load and trudge forward under duress. Their strength and fortitude in difficult times, in barren conditions, could be an inspiration to us. They have anticipated and are prepared for tough times. We should keep this in mind, as the future is uncertain.

This is not to say that we should put these individuals on a pedestal. Nor would they want that. They are very realistic in their appraisal of their own limitations and capabilities, and are not prone to vanity or self-importance. They are straight-faced and responsible. They have a deep, critical-thinking, analytic approach to life. They are not known for being highly excitable or emotionally expressive. But they are sensitive, have a keen sense of justice, and feel terrible when they realize they've been thoughtless or impolite. This makes them capable of being loyal, steady, trustworthy partners. But they also tend to spend a considerable amount of time deliberating before committing to any action. This can sometimes make them appear stuck in inaction. The truth is, they prefer no action to wrong action. This is not necessarily a bad thing; moving fast in the wrong direction is not progress.

Individuals with a predominance of this adaptive strategy tend to adhere to a general philosophy that might be characterized as, "Keep your head down and your nose to the grindstone." Just do whatever chores are in front of you, get by, and don't expect much. Life is a grinding treadmill in an oppressive system, but you do what you need to do to survive. In the workplace, these people are not management material, as they tend to lack the necessary political savvy, tact in their critiques, and cheerful demeanor that are traditionally considered good people skills. They couldn't care less. They're there to get their job done, period. "Is cheerful in my job description?" They're well suited to being long-term, routine-chained civil servants.

At the extreme end of the spectrum, individuals laboring through life under the weight of these conditioned patterns can sometimes become quite depressed and pessimistic. Their dark view of life, disappointment with self and others, and cynical appraisal of the future can lead them into a hopelessness corner that can be difficult to be around or draw them out of. They can be a "downer" and seem to find comfort in validation that their negative assessment is realistic and correct—"See … the glass really *is* half empty." It's hard to convince them that just because the world is going to hell in a handbasket doesn't mean they have to be unhappy. OK, I guess that is a pretty weak argument. But the point is, they don't *want* to be happy. They don't *want* to be different. They don't *want* to be cheerful or ambitious. They just want you to accept them the way they are (and accept that their view is more realistic than yours). If they feel pressured, their self-esteem collapses and they can become quite depressed. This is not a good thing. And not something you'll want to deal with. They can slip from their characteristic chronic, low-grade depressive orientation, into a full-blown episode of withdrawal from life: feeling worthless, helpless, defeated, without energy, and possibly suicidal—"What's the point?" Their characteristic defense of hunkering down and enduring the stress has (temporarily) failed. They've become overwhelmed. Keeping them safe and showing acceptance and care will probably (hopefully) make such episodes short-lived and infrequent. They don't need a lot. They don't demand a lot. They just want to feel accepted and appreciated for who they are—moderately miserable, but realistic.

If they get this respectful acceptance, they won't need convincing that things need to change. They can easily be incorporated into the mass of humanity that will be required to join forces for the transformation of society in steering our collective course toward a more sustainable and just global community.

Sociopathic

When Adventurous becomes Antisocial

Sociopath doesn't seem like a very kind label to pin on someone. And it's not. But then sociopathic behavior isn't particularly noted for its kindness, either. Tough and adventurous, yes. But kind? Not really. In fact, at its extreme end of the spectrum, this character type can be very *un*kind—ruthlessly aggressive, deceitful, manipulative, and downright dangerous. Still, it's also important to keep in mind that underneath these difficult behavioral patterns, ones that have been conditioned by cultural mistreatment, lies a human being capable of cooperation and caring.

In its milder, better-behaved forms, individuals with this character type are the ones we count on to "blaze the trail" into the unknown, where most of us fear to tread. They are the explorers whose voyages sought and found new lands to conquer and, unfortunately, conquered them instead of striving to more respectfully and cooperatively blend our culture with theirs. For better or worse, they are likely to be the captains of industry, military, and politics. They don't mind a rough-and-tumble competition because they are confident that they will come out on top—and they usually do. They have a bold, "no fear" approach to life. They take on any dare and thrive on the risk as much as the reward. They will stand up to anybody. It takes a certain rugged type to keep up with them in their pursuit of excitement. And if you should perish in the process of trying to keep up with them in some impulsive, high-risk situation, they will move on without much regret or experience of loss. You made a choice and it didn't work out—"Sorry." Just like that, they're on to the next adventure.

At the more dysfunctional end of this spectrum, a "lack of conscience" is the popular way of describing their ability to harm others without remorse. Prisons are filled with individuals bearing these adaptive patterns because, quite frankly, nobody really wants them for a next-door neighbor. They steal, lie, cheat, and are willing hurt anyone who confronts them. They aren't really interested in society's rules. They were too-often mistreated when they were young, and so, have adopted a stance in life that says, "Others didn't care about me, so why should I care about anybody else? I'll take what I want—and I want it *now*."

This makes them tricky to deal with, even in milder forms. In relationships, they will gladly use anyone willing to accept a victim role in relation to them. And they know just what to say to get self-sacrificing others to play along. They're unlikely to ever settle down and be a steady, reliable partner. Fortunately, they do seem to mellow somewhat with age. They might still be a little "slippery" in the integrity department, but somewhere around middle age they tend to become less driven toward risky behavior and begin to recognize that the younger "gun slingers" out there can and will "kick their ass" if provoked. They know they *were* a young gunslinger.

In the time of great changes that lies ahead, individuals with this character strategy are likely to come out on top of whatever scramble they find themselves in. Don't cross them, keep an eye on your stuff, and watch the direction in which they move. They're likely to uninhibitedly go for and exploit their best chances of survival and may, in that process, point the way toward a practical solution to a critical situation, even if it *is* pursued on the basis of short-term individual gain or is ultimately unsustainable. Then again, if their antisocial tendencies are tempered by other, more sociable character traits, this type of person could emerge as a bold, local leader of a cooperative economic enterprise that helps usher in a new era of commerce that is more equitable and sustainable. Every individual is different, and all are capable of change and growth. Just make sure you're not being duped and led to betray your own core principles about what is ethical and sustainable.

Helper-Victim

When Thoughtfulness becomes Self-Defeating

At their best, individuals with a predominance of this character strategy function as the glue that holds society together. They are the good citizens that volunteer, both formally and informally, to make sure that others are taken care of. They "get" what it means to be a community and what it means to be one's brother's and sister's keeper. They enjoy the feeling of security and belonging that results when they give of themselves. There is a place for them—but it isn't at the top or in the limelight. It's behind the scenes making sure that the gathering, whatever it is, is a welcoming and nourishing experience for all who attend. They live to serve and love to give. And, truth be told, they actually feel a little lost and uncomfortable if they don't have a place to put others' needs ahead of their own. They like to feel attached to a larger, stronger person, group, or cause.

These folks make great "worker bees" and are happiest when they are being helpful and serving others. They can be extremely humble and generous—a definite asset to any organization. They tend to be trustworthy, hard-working, loyal, considerate, and nonjudgmental toward others. They require very little (but some) appreciation. What they don't want is *public* recognition. They're uncomfortable being the center of attention or being put in a position where they appear ambitious, competitive, or prideful.

But there is a fine line beyond which selfless altruism can become self-defeating. Their self-sacrificing behavior can sometimes feel clingy. In moderation, an imbalance between giving and taking can result in a satisfying, stable relationship because both the giver and the taker are comfortable with it. But when the taking is done without consideration or decency, without occasional acknowledgment and appreciation, or when the giving is blind to the fact that others sometimes enjoy giving also, and the inability to accept creates a sense of guilt in the other, then it has gone too far. At that point, the desire to be connected through giving and self-sacrifice has become self-defeating. It places an unwelcome burden of obligation on the other person that can feel "clingy" or anxious, eliciting a desire to withdraw. The attempt to achieve acceptance through giving has failed.

Also potentially problematic is when their tolerance of others and their long-suffering nature results in being naïve interpersonally. They would probably benefit from being a little more suspect about the motives of others. Their wide-eyed innocence can get them into trouble—as givers—with people who too willingly take advantage of them. Their submissive, forgiving inclinations make them easy targets for those with sociopathic patterns (takers) who easily use them and hurt them without remorse.

At an extreme, individuals with this style become martyrs—working themselves to exhaustion, living a thread-bare existence, and suffering deep disappointment at not being recognized by ungrateful others for all that they do. They might become depressed, stressed-out, and feel unworthy and resigned to a disappointing life—despite how hard they try to please others. A little self-assertion and learning to say "No" would go a long way for these individuals. They need to be encouraged to speak up if they feel they are being treated unfairly.

Don't count on them to take an unpopular stand in front of a crowd. But when working behind the scenes for social change, they can be great affiliates to have on your team. They are respectful, reliable, sincere, competent, undemanding team players who can handle routine drudgery without complaining. We're all lucky to have them in our lives and it's all-too-easy to overlook their contributions. While they may become flustered by compliments and say, "Oh, it's nothing. You don't have to thank me," they do in fact need to know that you notice and appreciate them. So, be sure to thank them—in private.

Victor-Victimizer

When Strong Leadership and Healthy Aggression become Scary and Sadistic

At the more welcome end of the spectrum, individuals with a predominance of this adaptive pattern have a take-charge attitude that can be put to service for the greater good. They assume command and wield power with confidence. Strong and driven by nature, they are effective at getting the job done —practical, goal-oriented, ambitious, and self-disciplined. They never back away from a fight and are good to have on your side during difficult times. They thrive within traditional hierarchical power structures where the lines of authority are clear—especially when they are at the top.

They like to be "the boss" and expect others to follow their lead and take orders. And as long as no one steps out of line or challenges them, they can be benevolent—generous and supportive—as well as interesting and exciting to work for. But "cross swords" with them, and you'll wish you hadn't. Their need to dominate can go beyond a self-interested, sociopathic exploitation of others, to a sadistic pleasure in seeing competitors suffer degrading humiliation in front of others.

These are tough, forceful, "gutsy" leaders and they make sure others know it before challenging them. Intimidation gains them a psychological advantage, but they are also quick to back it with ruthless action. They don't let anything stand in their way and thrive in dog-eat-dog competitive environments where there is a winner and a loser. They are not easily deterred from clawing their way to the top. They don't allow emotions, relationships, or the need for rest to stand in their way. They will prevail.

Their actions are bold and effective, not inhibited by fear. They don't waste time feeling blue or sentimental. They are not squeamishly dissuaded by danger or gore, from relentlessly moving toward their goals. They charge to the front of the battle scene, rise to the challenge, and seem to even enjoy the combat. They have the "stomach" for it. They can make tough decisions, which makes them effective leaders in situations where lives must be sacrificed (e.g., war, emergency medical triage, corporate layoffs, lending foreclosures, political power brokering, etc.).

In a grudge match with a past competitor, or if they feel disrespected or "stung" by disloyalty, they might go beyond simply defeating the other and reasserting their dominance; they may become vengeful and punishing.

If you find yourself in a conversation across the divide with a person like this, you'll do well to *not* evoke an angry response. If they become aroused, don't get in their face or vent your anger back at them. It's generally better to back off and let things cool down before continuing. They will respect a strong, assertive stance as long as it's backed by reason, not emotion, and as long as it doesn't come at them as a personal challenge. If you find yourself feeling confronted, make an effort to avoid a win-lose situation. Don't insist on your way over theirs. Don't "defeat" them. They won't tolerate losing without seeking revenge.

Try instead to find a compromise that allows them to maintain a feeling of superiority, by your offering to give up something that is important to them in the negotiation, if they might allow a much-less-significant option in trade. Help them see how it will benefit them. If they feel as if they are coming out on top, you'll be more likely to get what you want. They need to see what's in it for them. If they can see an advantage or increase in power for themselves, they will likely become effective leaders for change at a high level within the current socio-economic structure. Circumstances will probably become more problematic for them if and as society shifts toward a less-hierarchical, more cooperative system. Either way, they are probably destined to play a dominant role over those who are less aggressive. Working to help them aim their ambition in the right direction is critical and worth the effort. It can be done.

Passive-Aggressive

When "Relaxed" Drives Everyone Else Crazy

"OK, I'll do it. Don't worry."

"Oops, I forgot again. Sorry."

"Relax! You're so uptight."

So it goes with some individuals. This character type appears unruffled while everyone around them is exasperated by their laid-back attitude.

At the mild end of the spectrum, individuals with a predominance of this style are on a leisurely stroll through life and can be quite easy going. They take care of their responsibilities, but just minimally. They'll usually do what they have agreed to, but not much more. They're definitely not "Type A" driven individuals. And they're not about to let anybody make them feel guilty about it or keep them from enjoying themselves at their own pace. Their time is *their* time. Not the boss's. Not the organization's. Not yours. They expect others to respect their rights to do whatever-the-heck they want to do with their "free" time. It's *their* free time. They're not particularly ambitious and that's just fine with them.

If pushed, they *will* resist and can be quick to point out the "unreasonable demands" and "excessive busy-ness" of others. They have no problem saying "No." In their view, it's fine if others want to succumb to the irrational cultural indoctrination of an unsatisfying work ethic, but not them—"No thanks. Not interested."

At the more extreme end of the spectrum, their "forgetfulness" and procrastination can become a persistent, indirect way of expressing their angry resistance at those who push them to conform and perform. They back themselves into a corner by being contrary, oppositional, uncooperative, late, negative, quarrelsome, and just plain stubborn. Their nit-picking argumentativeness wears others down and gets "oppressors" to eventually give up. This is what they wanted all along—"Just leave me alone and let me do my own thing. I don't tell you how to live *your* life, do I?" If others don't back off and these individuals continue to feel pushed and exploited by authority, they can become scornful and a real Human Resources department nightmare. They will entrench themselves and do just the very minimum to avoid being fired. Those who try to punish them will pay by having a minimally-functioning cog in their bureaucratic machine.

Such obstructionist behavior can be quite detrimental to an organization's functioning—sabotaging months of co-workers' efforts by missing a crucial deadline or being "sick" at a critical juncture. Co-workers in these situations end up feeling "burned" and frustrated by the chaos that ensues, while the passive-aggressive individual claims to be misunderstood and unappreciated. Their apathy and indifference to the crisis drives people around them crazy.

It's not that they are "cold" or uncaring interpersonally. In fact, they desire and enjoy closeness. But they will never be "owned" and are not likely to let anyone take advantage of them. They do, however, experience a dilemma in relationships. Their underlying need to be taken care of is in conflict with their need for independence. They're afraid that their dependency will result in being exploited by those in authority. Their neediness, along with their inability to directly express anger, makes them conflicted about how entwined to become with others. When they start to feel close, they find their dependent longings beginning to emerge. This makes them feel anxious. Their characteristic defense against this anxiety leads them to become passively aggressive and resentful toward the needed "other" in order to regain some distance and retain enough autonomy that they don't feel in danger of being controlled.

They'd be glad to have you join them in their pursuit of pleasure, as long as you don't require them to adapt to *your* inclinations. They don't need to be alone. However, if you press them on how unfair it feels to always have to do what *they* want, they might acknowledge it and feel some regret, but in the end, they will do what *they* want, even if it means doing it without you.

When you find yourself communicating across the divide with one of these individuals, it's usually not problematic as long as you make no demands on them to be different than they are. They are fine with letting you be who you are, have your own opinion, do whatever you like to do with regard to sustainability. And they might even be willing to listen, as long as it doesn't interfere with their free time too much. Don't expect them, however, to make any changes to please *you*. It's OK to talk with them about what you think is important. But don't expect them to pick up the pace because of the urgency of the challenges we face as a civilization. Until it disrupts their pursuit of happiness, change is not likely to be of much interest. If you press them, you probably won't be seeing much of them again. They will disappear from your life. If you are in a work situation and the changes you are requesting are a requirement of their job, then you will need to be very specific about what needs to be done differently (e.g., photocopies on *both* sides from now on, recycle used office paper *here*, etc.). And, if they keep "forgetting" or being "careless," you might try pulling them aside (not in front of others) and confronting them gently by asking if they are upset or angry about the required change.

It will probably also help if you find some things that you genuinely appreciate about them, and let them know about *those* things. They enjoy feeling like they're pleasing others by what they are already doing—just by being who they *are*.

Super Sensitive

When Sensitivity becomes Avoidance

"Hey, wanna come to the big party over at Mike and Janelle's? It's gonna be a blast! They're gonna have a live band and all the folks from the dance club are bringing their friends too!"

"Nah, that's alright. I'll pass."

"You sure? It's gonna be great?"

"Nah, I'm fine. Thanks. I'll pass."

Individuals with a predominance of this character type don't necessarily need to be alone. In fact, they are quite capable of enjoying emotional closeness and care very deeply about those they feel close to. It's just that they don't need a lot of friends or excitement to be satisfied. They usually feel uncomfortable in large groups and secretly, behind their polite façade, can't wait for such gatherings to be over. Escape from anxiety is one of their primary motivations in life. They're quite content to stay at home, read a book, work on one of their solo projects, or maybe visit with a life-long friend over a quiet supper. Maybe.

They are most comfortable with what is familiar and enjoy their small, comfortable life with a few close relationships. They are reserved and polite when meeting new people, but have a somewhat stilted self-conscious demeanor. They never want to appear inappropriate or hasty to pass judgment. Even long-time friends sometimes have to guess at what's going on inside them. They mask their underlying anxiety (they worry about everything), their interpersonal insecurity (they doubt themselves in the presence of others), and their feelings of vulnerability (they are easily hurt by criticism), with a characteristic politeness and quietness that leaves others unsure of where they stand. They need the approval of others to feel good about themselves. It matters to them what other people think of them. If they feel like they have "screwed up" somehow, they pull back ashamedly into their silence and go away to reflect on how they can do better. If, after quite a long time, they feel genuinely accepted and emotionally safe with someone, they are capable of loosening up (somewhat) and being genuinely warm, spontaneous, affectionate, loyal, and generous. They are most confident and comfortable with their small, close group of friends or immediate family.

Sometimes they are involved in individual creative pursuits (e.g., as artists, writers, gardeners, etc.) and can be quite imaginative and skilled at their craft. But they don't have any interest in receiving public recognition. They might, if they feel emotionally secure, share their latest creation with their closest friend. Or, maybe not.

In terms of their daily life, the Zen way of "chop wood, carry water" suits them well. They are comforted by the routine and like to know what's expected of them. They tend to dive vertically deeper into whatever interests them, rather than spreading their interests horizontally into new areas of discovery. They are more drawn to exploring "inner space" than "outer space" and can be quite knowledgeable and insightful about the nuances of their explorations. Underneath that well-mannered mask lies an interesting individual.

They are worriers, perhaps by nature, but also by conditioning, and like to be prepared. Not so much in a paranoid (guns and gold) way, but more in the hopes of never finding themselves in an embarrassing situation that could have been avoided by being better prepared—"Uh, could I borrow some batteries?" They can be a little compulsive in trying to account for every eventuality because of this fear of being caught off guard, but are generally more comfortable feeling that they have thought everything through and made preparations so that "If this happens, then I will do that."

These individuals learned to be self-reliant because, typically, they couldn't trust the parental and other older authorities in their life (including siblings) to protect them emotionally. They were often shamed into compliance, humiliated, and made to feel inadequate. They never want to have to rely on others again. Except they do want to. And therein lies the conflict they live with. They want closeness but fear it. They are lonely in their aloneness.

At the extreme end of the spectrum, their need for emotional self-protection can lead to avoidance of interpersonal environments to such a degree that it results in impaired social and occupational functioning. What might be a fairly common genetic predisposition toward social anxiety becomes a behavioral habit of avoidance with very real adaptive consequences. Over time, they may become depressed, or addicted to alcohol, which they use to reduce their anxiety.

It's important, when talking with them about the multiple, converging challenges that we face as a civilization, to keep in mind their propensity for worry. Too much "doom and gloom" will leave them traumatized and paralyzed. It's better for them to receive clear messages about the best ways to prepare and participate in the Great Turning that we are all undergoing. In this way, they can maintain a useful perspective rather than shrinking away from the challenges and hiding because they feel weak or helpless. To their credit, they can then be counted on as reliable and effective community members to at least have their own situation organized as things come unraveled. You just need to accept their tendency to withdraw and become stiff when others are around, and remember to not push them too fast. They can learn, with some encouragement and reassurance, to take small steps toward community involvement. But if you see them clam up or offer some last-minute excuse—"I don't feel well"—don't attack or push them, simply ask if they're feeling nervous, and reassure them that it will be alright and that others like them. In order to keep them from playing smaller and smaller in life, they need encouragement to "feel the fear and do it anyway."

It's important to help them recognize that imperfection doesn't necessarily mean that they will be rejected or harmed emotionally—it makes them human. They need to and *can* grow to accept their own shortcomings, and accepting that disagreements can and do occur between people who genuinely like each other. It's unrealistic to believe that people who care for each other will never feel angry with one another. It's also true that anger doesn't have to be dangerous, which is what they fear. This is what they need to learn. Anger can be a source of power for doing good in the world. It's OK to take a strong stand for what you believe is right. They have a contribution to make—but it needn't be on the podium in a public-speaking capacity. They'll likely respond to your approval for steps in the right direction, if it's not too much too fast. And lucky you, if they do. You've made it into their inner circle, where their warm, loyal friendship will be a blessing in your life and community.

Fuzzy Thinking

When Unique becomes a Little Too Eccentric

"Hey, what're ya doin' there? Trying to swat flies in slow motion? Or some sort of Tai Chi moves?"

"Oh … hi … no … I'm gathering crystallized energy molecules from the cosmic fallout into my aura … it's … you know … that time … when my planet's in retrograde and the dream elements converge to transmute all that exists into ancient wisdom … I'm a vegetarius you know … and it's important … it happened in a past life, too."

Sometimes individuals with this character style seem, uh … a little "off the deep end." They don't always experience the same double-blind-study-with-large-random-sample reality that comprises the conventional "consensus" most of us inhabit. But that doesn't mean they are bad people, or that they should be feared or excluded. They just don't always pay attention to the same data as most other people, and they don't generally travel the same prescribed paths through life.

At their best, these individuals exude originality and vision. They tend to live "between realms," gravitating toward their own unique inner/spiritual universe, and probably account for the lives of many historical mystics. Their odd lifestyle, full of eccentric rituals and mannerisms, makes most people "roll their eyes" and makes enough people uncomfortable that these individuals generally have relatively few close relationships. But they are not loners by choice. They like people and they know that others think they're weird. This makes them sad, but not enough to conform to ideas or directions that come from outside of themselves.

They can be quite astute at recognizing and labeling what's occurring interpersonally—to the point of creating discomfort in those around them because of their lack of adherence to social conventions about *not* saying what's really going on. The truth sometimes doesn't allow others the dignity of hiding behind their social facades. Individuals with a predominance of this character style don't feel compelled to play along with the charade. This backfires in many contexts (e.g., work environments) where some semblance of role behavior is assumed.

If they are able to keep their feet on the ground enough to interface effectively with others, the lack of conventional limitations on their thinking may lead them to conceptualize truly innovative solutions to problems which elude hard-working, square-thinking types. It's possible they could provide useful insights for the challenging times that lie ahead. Or, they could be off dancing to their own beat on the fringe, quite literally. Either way, they're not likely to be problematic to progressive efforts unless they repeatedly careen the discussion off course into non-productive tangents about metaphysics.

They tend to be drawn to New-Age gatherings and activities where they find relative acceptance for their peculiar beliefs and interests, but are not likely to join any group or commit to future participation that might require compliance with rules or protocol. They function best when they can do things their own way. If a work environment (or cultural context) lacks tolerance for their idiosyncrasies, they will tend to drift off (or be fired) and seek more "space" to pursue their current interests. They can usually contain their eccentricity for a while, but eventually it leaks out in little ways. Those in the "straight" world around them come to think of them as "odd ducks." This hurts their feelings and results in their (generally quiet) departure.

Their search goes on. They do best with a part-time work niche that provides enough sustenance that they can be themselves. They can cope with performing an undemanding routine task as long as it doesn't require a lot of pressure to conform. But they're not particularly ambitious, and can become irritable if they feel criticized for not doing things the right way (i.e., not being "normal"). The best situation, from their perspective, would be one which supports complete, uninhibited expression for their creativity. This is not to be for most.

As their life circumstances shift, so does their perception of reality. They continually try new religions, new therapies, new herbal remedies, and so forth. They seek and seek—sometimes to the point of losing touch with reality. Floating in a groundless universe that can leave them with more problems than they can manage—they lose their cognitive bearings, don't know how to understand or explain the world around them anymore, feel anxious, and may experience psychotic-like symptoms (e.g., inappropriate emotional reactions—such as laughing at something that's not funny, believing the person on the TV is talking to *them* personally, and so forth).

However, they are not schizophrenic, and these sorts of extreme exaggerations of their adaptive style are generally short-lived. They are, in fact, quite resilient. They'll fairly quickly come up with some mystical explanation for the disruption in their life, stumble onto a new belief system that holds interesting unexamined premises to explore, and just like that, they're back on the path (or at least *a* path) again.

When talking across a divide with individuals of this type, it's important to remember that they are not interested in conforming to *anybody's* ideas, no matter how progressive or alternative. Don't pressure them to accept *anything* on faith. It matters only if *they* believe it. They are true living phenomenologists. Experience is everything. If they experience it, it's the truth, no matter what anybody else says. If whatever is being said doesn't fit their immediate experience, it's perceived as simply other people, the culture, and so forth, trying to force them to conform. They aren't interested. And, don't expect them to join your group. They don't tend to swerve their life course to accommodate others. They're going *their* way, and their way changes quite readily. But that doesn't mean they can't enjoy interacting with you, as long as they feel accepted for who they are. Accept their uniqueness and know that it takes a lot for them to interact in a group with relative normality. Don't pressure them to be different than they are. Allow them to go *their* own way when they need to. But listen, also, to their feedback, because it can sometimes be quite accurate and helpful in its uniqueness. This is their gift. This is what they bring to the dialogue. Value it for what it is, and learn to tolerate the quirkiness. If you do, they might just drop in again with another gem for consideration.

Loyal

When Devoted becomes Dependency Without a Self

At the well-functioning end of this spectrum, individuals with a "loyal" character style can be quintessential team players. You want them in your life and on your team. Find them, meet them, invite them, befriend them, hire them, and marry them, if you can. They are honest, reliable, hard-working, helpful, caring, giving, loving, devoted, unpretentious people who make life wonderful for those around them. They're happy when you're happy.

Their consideration for other people's feelings and needs makes them invaluable in an organization, family, community, and so forth. They are relationship-oriented and prefer the company of others to being alone. They can make friends with almost anyone. They are flexible and willing to adapt their desires to those of others, and frequently do more than their share without complaining. They win the "plays well with others" award every time. They are cooperative and tactful.

They generally prefer following someone else's lead. They follow directions well, and don't enjoy making difficult decisions on their own. They especially don't like being in a supervisory position if disciplinary actions are required. Their inclination, in a situation like this, would be to meet with all involved, listen to everyone, and then seek the support of the group in making whatever decision is likely to please the most people.

Around the office, they are the ones who are likely to make sure that birthdays are remembered, that plans for the company picnic accommodate everyone, that holiday decorations offend no one, and that all the little details that make the work environment comfortable are attended to. They are thoughtful of others, polite, and agreeable. They work well within organizational hierarchies. They have no problem being respectful toward those in authority and find comfort in the institutional structure.

As we move toward the less-well-functioning end of the spectrum, it is sometimes the case that these individuals are, perhaps, too passive, submissive, and willing to please. Their reliance on others leaves them incapable of making important decisions on their own. Their dependency leads them to idealize others, and can lead to their being taken advantage of, especially by those with antisocial or sadistic tendencies.

Their desire to avoid conflict can sometimes result in turning any criticism against themselves, an excessive need for reassurance, and "clingy" behavior. They can become unsure of themselves and struggle with taking initiative. This can be exasperating for those they are trying to please. They'll do *anything* to forestall the end of a relationship, for fear of being alone, and they tend to become depressed when alone. When a relationship ends, they are quick to find another. They need to be attached in order to maintain their equilibrium. They feel much happier and more effective when securely connected. But it would actually support their growth and development, as individuals, if they were able to be a little more autonomous. They need to strengthen their sense of individual identity. And it would help strengthen them to stand alone, for a while, between relationships, to learn to make decisions on their own, and manage their own life rather than filling the void as quickly as possible.

When talking across the divide with these individuals you'll most likely find that there *is* no apparent divide. They will probably say whatever it is they think you want to hear. This is not good for them. And it is not good for the development of collective wisdom. They need to be encouraged to find and express their own voice, their own genuine concerns and opinions. It needs to be OK for them to sometimes agree, and sometimes disagree. They need to get beyond the "we think this, and we are voting for that" mentality, where their opinions and views are shaped by, and submerged into, those of the dominant people in their lives.

Social evolution, at this critical juncture, requires that all minds be on board, and that everyone is thinking clearly, and for themselves, so that our collective wisdom can guide us to make good, rational choices about how to proceed. They have good minds. They're not helpless, even if they fear they are. They just need to feel like the world won't end if they take a stand that differs from that of the person they are talking to. They need to be encouraged to think, decide, and act for themselves—as separate, individual adults. They won't be much help in spreading the consciousness of sustainability if they keep adapting what they say and think to those with opposing, non-progressive, fear-and-greed-based, self-interest, and profit-driven opinions.

With support and encouragement from the progressive community, and perhaps a little assertiveness training, these folks can be great emissaries. This is, perhaps, their best role in the Great Turning. They are really good at making others feel accepted and cared about, regardless of their politics or opinions. They can establish connections across the divide that make it feel safe to come together for dialogue. They can help bring about convergences where haughty "greens" put aside their snobbish criticisms and listen to their fellow humans with sincere interest and a desire for understanding. This will be necessary for finding a path forward that honors and meets the needs of those who feel differently. The data don't add up the same way for everyone, and these individuals have a gift for not making anyone feel bad or wrong for how they view our current circumstances. They continue to love people, and this may turn out to be one of our most needed sentiments in the decades ahead. They're not likely to be the ones arguing points of differentiation, but everyone at the meeting will feel genuinely welcomed and accepted by them, and as comfortable as possible being part of the community.

Loner

When Solitary becomes a Snail-Eye Strategy

Did you ever play with a garden snail as a kid? Remember how its eyes are located at the ends of those long tentacles on its head. So tempting to touch— but when you do, it slowly withdraws inward, back into its head, and hides. If you wait, after a few moments, it will start slowly reemerging from its hiding place and looking around again, hoping to not encounter another brush with danger. If you touch it again, those out-coming eyes will once again reverse direction and withdraw back into the seeming safety of the head, trying to fit as much as possible under a too-small shell. Now you'll have to wait longer before it ventures back out into the world. So it is with some people. Even the slightest brush with interpersonal contact can send them back into themselves, withdrawing into solitude. The briefest eye contact and a pleasant "Hello" from the cashier can be too much. It might be the most direct contact they've had in a week. And it's plenty.

It's not necessarily that they don't *like* people—it's that these individuals don't *need* people in the same way most of us do. They actually prefer being alone. They don't require companionship or someone to share their feelings with. This is different than the Super Sensitive type who wants, but avoids, interpersonal contact because of their fear of rejection. Individuals with this Loner style are more indifferent, in some ways. They seem happier living a solo life and don't necessarily feel lonely. The truth is, they don't really feel *much* at all. They spend a lot more time "thinking" than "feeling" and this can be frustrating to those who might consider it withholding of their emotions. But not everybody experiences emotions in the same way. Some feel more deeply and passionately. Others feel less intensely. And it doesn't bother them (emotionally) as long as others let them just be the way they are. Pushing for greater involvement and demanding that they be more emotionally responsive only backfires. They will pull away from what feels like entanglement and go hide—the "snail eye" pulls back in.

At the mild end of the spectrum, as long as their cognitive functioning is intact, their capacity for solitude makes them well-suited to endeavors that require isolation, for example, remote arctic monitoring stations, forest fire surveillance towers in roadless areas, endless hours in a laboratory pursuing esoteric scientific knowledge, and so forth. Under circumstances like these, their dispassionate observations and intellectual insights can be appreciated by society. The clarity of their insight stems, in part, from the fact that their observations are not colored or clouded by their emotional state. This is the archetypal reclusive genius.

As this character strategy becomes more extreme, however, the solitude might result in secondary problems from the lack of social feedback that keeps us all a little bit "on our toes." When we look in the mirror, we tend to imagine how others might see us, and that influences our presentation in life. Not so with these individuals. In fact, their indifference to the feedback of others may become so pervasive that they have difficulty fitting in with society. At the extreme, they tend to drift off and live where minimal contact with other humans is required. They don't pick up on interpersonal cues about when it's their turn to speak or other rules of etiquette. Their lack of basic social skills can make them appear rude, which they're not, necessarily. But the result can be harsh rejection and ostracism by those whose feelings are hurt by their lack of reciprocation or who are frightened by their differentness. In typical fashion, they don't respond to social rejection with anger or hurt, they simply go away—the "snail eye" pulls back in.

When talking to these individuals, it's important to respect their need for autonomy and privacy. Recognize that emotional contact is exhausting for them. Don't expect (or need) them to be warm and responsive toward you— just accept them as they are. They will probably *not* be interested in getting more involved with whatever group or movement you're interested in. They're *not* interested in more closeness, being more engaged or belonging. So be careful to *not* be intrusive, lest you set off their withdrawal to solitude. That they're even in your presence is a big (uncomfortable) step for them.

They'll be more comfortable if you don't fill all the silences, too. Make it OK for them to just be there and observe, to not have to say anything, and to leave whenever they feel like it. In all likelihood, they are taking a lot in and thinking deeply about what they are observing. If you are quiet enough, for long enough (which is not easy to do as they can take an excruciatingly long time to respond) you might begin to notice subtle indications that something is brewing inside of them. If allowed to emerge, unhurriedly, it quite often reflects their clarity, based on deliberation, and can be taken as a sign of their caring about you and what's important to you. Little by little, like the snail eye, they might emerge from their shell and extend their presence into the room and your life—but ever so slowly and tentatively. Let that be OK.

Part One	Part Two	Part Three	Part Four

Part One

Why The Book?

The current cultural momentum is:

- unsustainable
- unsatisfying
- conditioned
- fear and greed based
- changeable, but...

- Personal Growth
- Moral Maturity
- Social Evolution
- Human Potential

Part Two

Three Things

Understand the person you are talking with:

- **Section One**
  their unique
  CHARACTER STYLE

- **Section Two**
  their
  CURRENT WORLDVIEW

- **Section Three**
  which
  EXISTENTIAL CONCERN
  they are struggling with

Part Three

Techniques

You might try:

- listening
- "between the lines"
- parallel their arguments
- question assumptions
- change the context
- stick to common ground
- applaud all steps
- other ideas...

Part Four

Examples

Imagine yourself in:

- An Awkward Event
- A Workplace Conflict
- Air Travel Delay

Section 2) Current Worldview

A SECOND THING TO KNOW AND KEEP IN MIND ABOUT THE PERSON WE ARE
communicating with is their current worldview. Let's begin by making a
distinction between "character type" and "worldview." For the purposes of this
book we are using the term "worldview" based, somewhat, on the Germanic
Weltanschauung concept, that is, a person's overall perspective from which
they see, interpret, and enter the world—where they're "coming from" in life.
Our use of the term, however, will also be influenced by those[1] who describe
worldview *not* as a static state, but as a continually evolving aspect of existence
progressing through various stages of psychological and moral development.
From this perspective, character might be considered a "type," whereas
worldview might be conceived as a "level" or "stage" along a developmental
continuum. The implication is that any "type" of individual can exist at any
"level" of development. Thus one's *character* type can be seen as a more
or less fixed set of adaptive capacities, whereas one's *worldview* represents
a temporary developmental stage of consciousness that has been reached.
Each level (worldview) seems to have its own qualitatively distinct pattern
of complexity, with its own associated modes of functioning, perceiving,
and understanding. We are all progressing, hopefully, along a path toward
"higher" levels of consciousness. This is what is referred to as "the evolution
of consciousness."

It might be said that a person's worldview goes beyond, surrounds, and
provides a context within which their characteristic ego-defense mechanisms
function. In our usage, a person's worldview includes their underlying/over-
arching philosophical stance in life—their deepest/highest core values. It both
includes and influences their attitudes, beliefs, perceptions, political orientation,
lifestyle, aesthetic preferences, priorities, and manner of speech, as well as
their cognitive and affective style. It's more than simply how they protect
themselves from anxiety as they navigate through life. It's their understanding
of life at its most essential level. Worldview is not just *what* a person thinks,
or even *how* they think, but *why* they think the way they do. Worldview

encompasses motivations as well as what is appealing and repellent. It influences how they view their self, how they view others, and how they view the world around them (e.g., friendly, hostile, meaningless, etc.) It is more fundamental than race, religion, nationality, or gender. It's what makes a fundamentalist a fundamentalist, whether they are Christian or Islamic.

It's important to understand that a person's worldview cannot be known by what they *say* they believe. It is their *behavior*—what they actually *do*—that reveals what they truly believe and the worldview from which they operate, regardless of what they say.

The impact of one's worldview on life choices cannot be easily side-stepped. It is the contextual (underlying/over-arching/surrounding) conception of how life *works*, how the *universe* works, one's cosmology and what being alive is all about. It's how we make sense of and ascribe meaning to life.

In an adaptive sense, worldview accounts for, and arises in relation to, current life circumstances. Somewhat akin to Maslow's[2] hierarchy of needs, more stringent and severe circumstances generally foster a more "primitive" worldview focused on basic survival needs, while easier life circumstances allow for the emergence of "higher" sentiments and aspirations. A person's worldview might be more or less congruent with the prevailing surrounding culture's worldview, but generally it arises in response to broad, real-life circumstances.

Technically speaking, there are as many worldviews as there are people. But, as with character types, there are also certain recognizable patterns that can be useful for classification and understanding. While some character types are more compatible with certain worldviews, any character type can be found existing within any worldview. (Even loosely organized tribal cultures have a version of the obsessive-compulsive, the flamboyant, and the fuzzy thinker.)

It's important to note that it is not just individuals who hold worldviews. Groups, organizations, and even whole nations can be understood as operating from, and existing under the influence of, a particular worldview. Similar to individual developmental sequences, worldviews evolve and adapt as circumstances change. Thus we see the rise of nations from loose bands of wandering humans to tribal groupings to warlord-dominated nations, to orderly-but-authoritarian conformist societies, to pluralistic civilizations. This progression tends to parallel the emergence of less rigid, broader, more sophisticated and complex worldviews among the individuals in those societies.

At this historic juncture, we find ourselves individually and collectively in need of "conscious evolution"—consciously deciding how we want to move forward as a global community, lest our baser instincts result in our own termination as a species. The assertion here is that we have the potential to "rise above" our reactive, impulsive, conditioned patterns that are based on fear and greed, and to reach for a future together that is based on generosity, compassion, cooperation, and reason.

The four worldviews presented in this book have been chosen because they tend to be both culturally common (in early twenty-first century North America) and problematic when attempting to communicate across the divide about progressive social change and sustainability from the progressive side of the dialogue.

---

[1] Beck, D. and Cowan, C. (1996); Csikszentmihalyi, M. (1994); Dowd, M. (2008); Gebser, J. (1985); Gilligan, C. et al. (1988); Graves, C.W. (1970); Kegan, R. (1982); Kohlberg, L. (1976, 1981); Korten, D. (2006); Loevinger, J. (1970, 1976, 1987); Wilber, K. (1996).

[2] Maslow, A. (1962, 1971).

PART TWO: THREE THINGS TO KNOW

Tribal

Our People—Our Ways

With the exception of native populations, in the developed world it's uncommon to think of people as affiliated with a tribe. Yet tribe-like loyalties exist in all socioeconomic strata, and in all ideological niches of contemporary society. The tribal nature of various clubs, groups, organizations, religions, companies, regions, and sports fans is evident if we look beneath the socialized surface presentation. While blood-lineage might not be required, there is still a strong, tribal sense of kinship or extended family where "belonging" contributes to one's sense of identity and a feeling of safety. Feeling connected to a "tribe" of like-minded folks can give life a sense of coherence, meaning, and purpose.

Safety and perpetuation of the group are two primary motivations for people with this worldview. There is safety in belonging. For example, living near or *with*, and gathering together with others of the same clan provides a sense of safety. Comfort, (or relief from anxiety), is found not only in proximity, but also in the sense of closeness that results from a merged identity ("we"), harmonious emotional resonance with each other, and well-understood rituals and routines.

Such bonding gives an often illusory sense that one's self (identity) is larger, more solid and secure, and that all hardships can be endured "as long as we stick together." For this, one is eagerly willing to subjugate individuality. The group becomes more important than the individual—one for all and all for one! Unfortunately, this "we take care of our own" mentality can too often become a form of nepotism that ends at the border of the clan, excluding the surrounding community. While individuals functioning within this worldview embrace the concept of collective interdependence, a common progressive value, it is usually narrowly framed as pertaining only to *their* particular reference group: family, organization, club, religion, nation, and so forth. This inward huddling as a group is generally stimulated and exacerbated by an underlying fear of an inability to cope and survive on one's own.

When external (environmental, social, economic) conditions become harsh, groups with this worldview can sometimes regress into a rigidified, fearful, superstitious stance, where "magical thinking" can supersede rationality. In hopes of appeasing some fearsome supernatural force, some individuals might resort to fairly primitive forms of thinking and ritual. Symbols may be displayed more prominently and speech may become ridden with forced, repetitive affirmations attempting to bolster denial-based defenses against anxiety. Some of this might look rather silly and be dismissed as childish. Nonetheless, superstitions do exist in the psychology of otherwise rational-appearing people. Witness the regressed behavior of certain people during calamitous times or when their favorite sports team is entering a particularly important contest.

In less-developed societies, the external appearance of this worldview might be quite different than in more developed societies, but the process is quite similar. For example, when a storm blows in it is not uncommon for the rain to be preceded by a period of gusty wind. In ancient times, observers of this phenomenon might have concluded that since the tree shook before the rains came, then shaking the tree will bring the rains and an end to our drought. Thus the tribe attempts to shake the tree in order to make rain.

In modern society, it's unlikely that you will find people shaking trees. Yet all sorts of "magical" (ungrounded in science) explanations are posited by certain groups for such phenomena as severe weather events, social decline, economic instability, and so forth. The proliferation of "end times" prophecies and the scapegoating of subgroups would be examples. In some cases, such views do not account for more basic, rational, well-understood cause-and-effect explanations. (This is not to say that science has the only, or the ultimate, answers.) But under that modern-day veneer, you might find that some individuals (and groups) are generally more focused on placating the supernatural to avoid punishment, than on taking rational actions to improve the human condition. The line between fantasy and reality becomes blurred. It goes beyond things like naming cars, wearing a rabbit's foot, or knocking on wood for good luck.

We see a more virulent form in the way some Americans regard the flag— a piece of cloth—as "sacred." To be sure, the U.S. flag represents some of the highest sentiments of humanity. And we are all indebted to those who have sacrificed for the freedoms it represents. But at another level, it's just a piece of cloth. A symbol is *not* the thing it represents. This is where the distortion lies. We value freedom and democracy—not cloth! Yet we find some people willing to fight and even *kill* those who would "desecrate" a piece of cloth. (Admittedly, some of those individuals desecrating the cloth can sometimes be excessively provocative and disrespectful in their behavior. But that's not the point here.)

In pre-developed societies, it is sometimes true that people with this world-view are "pre-literate" in the sense of not being able read. This makes them unable to take advantage of the accelerating, accumulating written knowledge of the developing world. But in industrialized settings, most people operating within this worldview know how to read. Still, their thinking continues to gravitate toward a non-linear mode of processing. They are more drawn toward simplified, symbolic stories and images as conveyors of "Truth" than toward critical thinking and analyzing data. This makes them extremely susceptible to the influences of corporate-sponsored media and Hollywood by those who understand how to use symbolic imagery and storytelling to convey values that rumble deep within the psyche. They are much more likely to resonate with a jingle or a logo than with written words.

Thinking, within this worldview, relies heavily on dichotomous simplifica-tion. You're either one of us, or you're not. You're either "fer" it or "agin" it. There are "good" spirits and there are "evil" spirits. Such black-and-white portrayals of reality leave much out of focus, and out of reach. Such in-group/out-group rigidity can be detrimental to the group's adaptive capacity in the ever-changing world. This slowness to accept change tends to isolate and separate the group in a modern pluralistic society, from the emergence of new knowledge that is occurring all around them at an ever-increasing pace. It can result in conflicts with neighboring groups who hold a more "advanced" worldview and no longer find it acceptable to rely on "magical" explanations for matters that affect "the commons." In some cases it may lead to eventual absorption by, rather than integration with, the surrounding culture. The larger contextual civilization may evolve beyond an ability or willingness to accommodate rigidly held customs that threaten progress. Over time, however, often via emancipated offspring or an influx of extended family members, exposure to the wider world will generally reveal the unsubstantial nature of some of the group's ways. Within-group challenges to the credibility of inflexible leaders by group members seeking "success" in the surrounding modern world can result in a dissipation of the group's cohesion and assimilation into the broader social context.

As long as things are going along harmoniously, individuals and groups with this worldview are not inclined to actively extend themselves toward others socially in order to increase their affiliations. They are content to stay within their group boundaries and worldview. So "crossing the divide" may be up to you. One of the best ways to reach and influence individuals with this worldview is through stories. Another way, if allowed, is through participation in their rituals. This, of course, would require the acceptance of their honored leader(s). Through this route, they might be invited to embrace the wisdom of both traditional *and* modern ways, where both seek a harmonious co-existence with nature. Belonging to the web of life and participating in its cycles in a more sustainable manner resonates with their interest in getting along with the forces of nature, as well as with modern environmentalism. Keep in mind, however, that they're less interested in the facts (data) about ecological systems, than the notion of safety through mutual reciprocity between people, and between people and nature.

Individuals and groups with this worldview value communal belonging because of the uncertainty of life. They can willingly live in cooperative inter-dependence, and understand that giving up some individual gain in order to help others endure difficult times is important because, ultimately, their own survival, and the persistence of the clan, may depend on their connectedness and reciprocity with others. As a species and a global civilization, it may turn out that individual survival increasingly depends on our collective ability to share, rather than compete violently for, the remaining limited resources. Broadening this worldview's communal tendency beyond their own limited reference group, to embrace the concept of a "global community" with relative social equity, is the challenge and the hope.

In regards to ecology, especially in less-developed parts of the world, the traditional stance of this worldview has been one of respect and fear of nature's power. They seek to blend harmoniously with nature. Traditional approaches worked well when human numbers were small in comparison to the bounty of natural resources surrounding them. But as populations have grown, and industrialization has hastened the pace of resource extraction, we tend to see short-sighted agricultural practices where, for example, forests, wildlife, watersheds, and fertile soils are being sacrificed for fast profits. In such cases, thousands of years of delicately balanced biological diversity and ancient wisdom are sometimes gone in a generation. A larger perspective is required to halt disaster.

When talking across the divide about such matters with people who are functioning within this worldview, it's important to understand and respect the internal social dynamics and customs of their group. They won't tolerate violation of their time-honored social structures. They have established connections, a decision-making process, and respected elders/leaders. Be careful to *not* minimize the importance of whatever taboos or rituals they invest with special meaning. And be extremely sensitive to their tendency to polarize around the in-group/out-group thinking mentioned above, lest you find yourself trying to communicate, ineffectively, from the outside. You'll get much further by figuring out and utilizing the within-group hierarchy of membership. Establishing a connection with a slightly more peripheral, extended family member as a liaison might be a good approach. Try connecting with someone who married into the family—and thus into the "tribe"— more recently. They have already been accepted. The group is much more likely to trust a message of change when it is delivered by one of their own. They also have an established process. Understand it and learn to work with it. After they've met among themselves, their accepted leader will most likely be the one to announce the decision for the group, and all will follow willingly. You might think it's unnecessary or unimportant, but they take their allegiance to this process, their elders, and traditional ways very seriously.

If they even suspect that you're not interested in trying to understand *their* "ways," they'll turn away from you. If they detect any hint of disrespect for whatever *they* consider sacred, you will be perceived as a threat and a risk invoking their tribal-warfare hatred. If you try to force them to change faster than they are ready, you will only stir up anxiety that will cause them to regress and pull inward more tightly and defend their known "ways" with deep vengeance.

They are more likely to respond positively to a message that has been approved and delivered by one of their respected leaders—one who has arisen from within the group, one whose leadership is followed without question. Making the effort to understand and respect their ways will make you, and your message, more attractive and acceptable. Appeal to their longing for safety, demonstrate respect for their connections with each other, and honor the importance of their traditions and authorities. This can help you gain a listening about the importance of social justice and environmental responsibility. Once they feel that their security needs have been met, and if they see that their respected elders and peers are "on board" with the required change, then it is likely that they will become agreeable and willing to participate in and contribute to the new way.

Might Makes Right
My Life—My Needs

"I'm getting mine, and nobody's gonna stop me. Life isn't fair. We're *not* all equal. Somebody's gotta be on top—and it's gonna be me." And likely it *will* be. People with this worldview put themselves first. They have little problem with the ideas of empire or exploitation—as long as they're among the ruling elites. And they usually are. If they're not, they soon *will* be, because they fight like hell to break free from any sort of submission or constraint put upon them by anybody or anything. They'd rather die on their feet than live on their knees, and they can be extremely ruthless and effective at eliminating competitors. Having successfully fought their way into a position of power, don't expect them to feel any guilt about being in the dominant position. After all, "might makes right" in this world.

It's possible that individuals with this worldview could become valuable compatriots in the tough times that lie ahead. But most likely, while you're looking for a trustworthy connection, they're just "in it" for themselves. Sure, they might help you plan and execute an effective resistance campaign for change. But don't expect them to extend a hand back to pull you to safety after they're in the clear. Their loyalty is likely to last only as long as their self-interest is involved. After that, it's "every man for himself." While this may seem callous, and often it is, remember that self-interest can be considered a strength of this worldview. It allows individuals to stand firmly against the pull for submission to the (regressive, less-effective tribal) ways of the group. It allows individuals to arise as leaders and find a better way forward.

Those with this worldview thrive in situations where chaos and anarchy turn civilized expectations upside down. There's a sort of social Darwinism at work in these circumstances, where uninhibited action takes the spoils. But where cooperation and consideration of others is required, those with this worldview can run into trouble. Their behavior might be *too* greedy, or *too* cruel and indifferent. Or, the people they are trying to dominate might not be quite as passive as they assume. Or, perhaps the oppressed are more aware of alternatives to submission (e.g., democratic process) than the oppressor had counted on. In these instances, those who are operating from such an individualistic worldview may find that being "tough" and "going it alone" is *not* the best strategy. They might discover that they actually *need* other people and a cooperative community in order to survive and thrive. (see sidebar on page 103) In this case, they may be willing to consider another angle, but will likely still be looking to gain whatever advantage is possible.

In general, this worldview encourages putting one's self before and above everyone else. It suits the more aggressive character types. It promotes egocentricity in the truest sense of being extremely identified with one's individual ego, and the ego's survival and satisfaction, as the central matters of life. Survival and power are key themes. Power *over* others is viewed as an acceptable necessity, as well as a source of meaning and pleasure in life. Society is seen as a hierarchy of strength. There is a pecking order. And in a world of "haves" and "have-nots," where the rich get richer and the poor get poorer, it's *good* to be a "have." This is justified by the belief that the "haves" deserve what they have because they are stronger, smarter, and more aggressive. They are willing to do whatever it takes to win, to gain the advantage, and to keep the upper-hand. This stance, backed by force, buys them respect among the more timid and intimidated masses.

Individuals with this worldview like respect. They *demand* respect. They do whatever it takes to gain and keep the fearful respect of others. In a group, organization, or society that is operating at this level of consciousness, individuals are rewarded for being street-smart and assertive. They strive to out-compete those who are more passive and less calculating—"The weak are downtrodden and exploited because, well … they're weak. Life is a jungle. Some are predators; some are prey. It's eat or be eaten. The have-nots deserve their lot in life because they are the lesser ones."

At its most extreme, sweatshops, even slavery, might be tolerated for personal gain, with indifference to the suffering of others. The underclass is held in its subservient status by making examples of some. Those who speak up about injustice or inequality risk punishment. The nail that stands up gets hammered down. The use of threats, coercion, even violence—whatever it takes to retain control and respect—can be justified within this mindset. This is one end of the spectrum.

On the more positive side, this worldview contributes to pushing society forward into new frontiers. Such individuals and groups tend to be action-oriented and courageous, unafraid of venturing into the unknown. They are not afraid of life, not afraid of others, and not afraid to stand or die alone. This allows them to rise above the huddled masses and pull society along in *their* direction. If harnessed for social good, this can be an asset for progressive social evolution. Too often, however, in the context of the current global economic system, their leadership ability is misspent on exploiting far-away peoples and places for personal gain, contributing to the unsustainable, profit-driven consumption of natural resources. But again, in its less virulent forms, this worldview can help spawn highly innovative strategies for change and adaptation. There is little feeling of obligation to tradition or established rules, and no unnecessary adherence to outdated customs. They tend to make the rules as they go and, in this way, can be effective leaders for those who prefer to follow. They lead with strength and are clear about their expectations of compliance. Be willing to work with them, to turn unhealthy expressions of aggression and greed into more pro-social sublimations, and their behavior might be shaped, by the application of carefully chosen reinforcement (rewards), toward increasingly positive, progressive social change. This would require that you (or whoever is undertaking the endeavor) be strong, unintimidated, and consistent in relation to them.

When talking across the divide with individuals operating from this worldview, it's safe to assume that they are thinking (if not saying directly)—"What's in it for me?" They're "on the take" and assume that everyone else is also. They don't see any altruism in life—"Everybody has their price." You need to offer, and deliver, something they want. They're not really interested in changing the world or contributing for the common good unless there's something in it for them. They want immediate gratification—some sort of payoff—*now.* They might have some interest in gaining the appearance of legitimacy through affiliation with you or a recognized institution that makes it possible for them to put behind their history of unsavory methods of attaining power. If you can find a way to invite them to a new power arena, and convince them that doing the "right thing" might bring them even more influence (and perhaps more pleasure, too), *then* they'll be more likely to consider your angle. For instance, they might be drawn to alternative energy technologies as a rapidly expanding market, if they feel as if they can gain some advantage for profit. If it makes them look good, too, it will have even more appeal. Just keep an eye on their labor practices. They're not beyond using bribes, kickbacks, payoffs, or indebtedness as a way of doing business that gets results—"What's wrong with an exchange of favors?" they ask. The answer is, of course, "Nothing, except when it turns into a racket of corruption and vendettas," as can sometimes happen under their rule. Not that they are bad people, but the rules of doing business within this worldview condone such practices as normal and smart competitive behavior.

When talking across the divide with these individuals, there is a fine line you must always be aware of between speaking with enough authority to command their attention, on the one hand, and never causing them to feel challenged or belittled—especially in front of others. Even more so if their character type has any tendencies toward paranoid, aggressive (victimizer), or sociopathic functioning. Always relate to them as though they are powerful and honorable, and know that they need to feel in charge and as if they are the ones "calling the shots" in order for them to consider compromising. They will respect strength, reputation, straight talk, and payoffs. If they detect any hint of weakness in your stance, it will merely activate their predator instincts. On the other hand, if you make any sort of implied threat, or if they feel humiliated or betrayed by you in any way, watch out—they *will* get you back and make you pay.

This worldview, regardless of individual character strategy, considers eliminating competitors to be a good thing. Also, it's not wise to make any promises you're not certain you can deliver on. If you fail to deliver, and thereby disappoint them, there will be negative consequences to endure. If you screw up somehow, don't whine or make excuses—just make it right, *now*, with deference and bonuses. They accept cash. And, it should go without saying, never try to con them. You can't beat them at their own game. They'll see right through your bullshit and set you up to hang yourself— "Gotcha!"

COOPERATION AS ADAPTIVE STRATEGY

In the era that lies ahead, we may find that the social, economic, and environmental challenges faced by humanity require collective, rather than individual, solutions. Individual survival may depend, increasingly, on our collective cooperation, generosity, and compassion as a species.

Evolutionary psychology suggests that the majority of human psychological mechanisms are adaptations to the environmental conditions of two million years ago, and that many individual, survival-oriented adaptations may now be "mismatches" for our modern circumstances. In other words, there might be a mismatch between our individualistic worldviews, and what will be required for future adaptation as a global community.

PART TWO: THREE THINGS TO KNOW

Order and Authority

Conformity and Rules

THERE'S SOMETHING COMFORTING ABOUT A WORLDVIEW THAT OFFERS A clear set of answers to life's big questions. Whether it's religious, political, or any other type of "ism" (including environmentalism) it somehow simplifies life to believe that all you have to do is follow the rules and good things will come your way. Just get in line, obey authority, work hard, and be patient. If you do this, rewards will one day be yours—eventually, maybe. At least that's what this worldview promotes, and what individuals with this worldview want to believe. And in many instances, they are correct.

This life-stance has done a lot to benefit both individuals and society-at-large. It brings order where chaos once reigned. Poor souls who felt "adrift without a rudder" find themselves "saved" and charting a new course. For example, those who have been hopelessly addicted to substances submit to a Higher Power, follow the (twelve) prescribed steps, and find stability and hope returned to their lives. Groups, organizations, and even nations that have been struggling under anarchy find a workable structure that brings productivity and prosperity to a large number of people. Conformity and consistency bring tangible results. What must be done, must be done. And while not everyone particularly likes their assigned role, there is, at least, an understanding and acceptance that the individual is less important than the whole, less important than the rules, and less important than the task to be accomplished.

In this worldview, people are cogs in a machine, regardless of their character type. Fulfilling one's role is one's destiny. Requiring people to sacrifice their individuality and work hard for "The Cause" builds character. It encourages a strong moral sense and good standing among those adhering to the "One True Way." This worldview provides a "rock" to which people can anchor their lives and help bring about a sense of civility and order. Self-interest and personal indulgence only exacerbate materialistic social decay (and the wasting of natural resources). According to this worldview, a much preferred way of organizing society, and *all* groups of people, is with clear hierarchies, in which everyone has, and knows, their proper place and job. Authoritarian leadership and a known chain-of-command bring welcome stability to many lives. There are detailed "marching orders" for all levels of society, and obedience to higher-ups is assumed.

At its best, this worldview cultivates honest, responsible, dutiful, charitable citizens. People genuinely feel a sense of moral obligation to each other and exhibit unwavering loyalty to the system, the organization, the faith, the cause, the movement—whatever they are identified with that provides direction in life. Empowered by a sense of righteousness, leaders within these groups rise and take charge. Life is organized into doable tasks which are assigned according to "worthiness" which, at its best, means based on things like ability, seniority, loyalty, sacrifice, and so forth. "Average" people find their niche and self-worth by subordinating their individual interests, and selves, to the prescribed "correct" behavior and "proper" protocol. Individuals want to be seen by others as dependable and productive members of their community, as "good team players." It's less important to "get-ahead" personally. This adherence to hierarchy results in a strong middle class, where people know and accept their station in life and do their jobs. And life rewards them fairly (enough) for their service and sacrifice. Individuals functioning from this worldview don't expect too much, and they don't get too much. But they do get enough to keep them happy, or at least pacified, and they enjoy a sense of stability and order in their lives—or at least this is what they are promised and what they aim for. (It seems to have worked better at various historical times than it does these days.)

In its idealized American Dream form, this worldview is populated by happy people living in communities where lawns are green, mowed, and weedless. Boundaries are made clear with manicured hedges and non-offensive, freshly painted, white picket fences. Driveways and garages are neat and tidy to passing neighbors, who are greeted with genuine positive regard. Laws are followed whether anyone is watching or not. There is peace and quiet on the block (and Neighborhood Watch signs posted). Traffic flows smoothly and there is a place for everyone. Holidays, patriotism, and home-team sports victories are celebrated and enjoyed with a real sense of belonging. People with this worldview are comfortable with themselves, comfortable with their lives, and have an enviable sense of assuredness that how they are living is the *correct* way to live—the way everyone should live—according to THE Higher Authority. They *know* where the path they are on is headed. Rewards lie ahead in return for a lifetime of duty and sacrifice. (Heaven? Gold watch and pension?) Their sense that the universe is understandable, predictable, and accommodating makes it possible for many to feel secure, and to extend their hospitality and generosity to others. They feel at home in the universe, enjoy a balanced, peaceful, orderly life, and pray that others will join them.

In its less pleasant manifestations, this worldview can be annoyingly self-righteous and rigid. It can lead to a dogmatic and intolerant stance where individuals become highly judgmental and tradition-bound, even fanatical at an unhealthy fundamentalist extreme end of the spectrum. Concern with order and control becomes compulsive, and zealotry draws sharp black-and-white distinctions between "good" and "evil." This can result in the use of exaggerated oversimplifications to attack and oppress others. The labels "conservative" and "liberal" become "fascist" and "commie." There's little room for consideration of gray areas. Compromise and "versions of truth" don't exist. Relativity is shunned. Absolutes are embraced.

At this less-reasonable extreme, people are categorized within a strict hierarchical social system. Everyone has their ordained place in the Grand Scheme according to their inherent worthiness. And, for the most part, fraternization across levels or classes is frowned upon. Too often these placements in the hierarchy have been made along politically and economically expedient racial, ethnic, gender, religious, and socioeconomic lines. People are expected to accept their rank, make the most of it, and be thankful. Convictions of the ruling class are imposed with punitive discipline. Condemnation and shunning are applied to evoke shameful submission. Guilt and fear of punishment under "The Law" bring about compliance to "Rightful Authority." Redemption is possible, but only with appropriate suffering and confession—"That's why they call it *work*" is the unempathetic motto of those who condemn the whining of underlings who were born into lesser stations according to the Divine plan. It is their destiny to grind away at difficult lives, toiling in service to "The System" while the profits flow up the socioeconomic ladder—the manifest destiny of the ruling class. It is God's will. The Puritan work ethic asserts that rewards come in the *after*life (or, in the case of low-level civil servants, at the end of a life of sacrifice). One must *accept* that fact, feel guilty for desiring more than one's lot in life, and get back to work.

In this worldview, the natural environment might be held in high esteem. Extremists aside, most individuals operating within this worldview genuinely desire to live a rightful life. They can easily embrace the concept of their role as stewards of "God's creation." Being a good boy- or girl-scout means managing nature's bounty with reverence and respect. That includes instituting and following appropriate laws and regulations to protect it. Using environmental legislation for the protection of endangered species and the management of natural resources is the "right" thing to do. Whistle-blowing to alert higher authorities where corruption is discovered is considered an honorable and courageous act. Everyone must play by the rules. That's what protection agencies are for. Fairness and doing what is "right" takes precedence over profit—for the most part.

But neo-liberal free-market capitalism, as an organizing principle for civilization, has been so heavily promoted by corporate-sponsored media, and with such compelling conviction, that this worldview has largely ingested at an unconscious level, the notion of profit-driven resource extraction as beneficial. This has become integrated into the belief system. This makes it possible to become so focused on the details of dutifully managing resources as commodities for "the economy" that the degradation and depletion of the resource itself is overlooked. In this scenario, corporate profiteers walk away leaving a mess for the rest of us to deal with. If and as it becomes more obvious what's really happening here, individuals with this worldview will represent a strong block of voters and activists for ecological sensibility. (Note the environmental victory of the Evangelical Climate Initiative—"What Would Jesus Drive?")

When talking across the divide with individuals who operate from this worldview, it is possible to appeal to their desire to do what is right. They respect what is truthful and charitable. They feel a sense of duty—as citizens, as stewards, as elders to future generations—to do the right thing. Self-sacrifice for a higher cause is a part of this worldview. And if their new cause becomes environmental sustainability, then they should be welcomed with open arms.

It's also helpful to recognize that many who hold dearly to this worldview were often raised in harsher circumstances than those in which they live today—their lives were less secure, less stable, and deprivation was their reality. Many were also held to unattainable performance standards. In some cases this has left them with a fragile underlying sense of self-worth (i.e., worthiness for *being* instead of *performing*). Attempting to broaden their worldview beyond their current firmly held belief that there is only One True Way can sometimes feel threatening or disapproving to them. This re-injury can cause them to withdraw from you and regress into a defensive stance with a "good/evil" split (i.e., the divide) between you and them, making you and your message "unsafe" to trust. Go slowly and sensitively.

Lastly, be sure to avoid any appearance of being "above" or disregarding any of the rules. Don't get caught trying to go around proper protocol, or gain special favor. There is very little tolerance, in this worldview, for anything that appears potentially sleazy or unfair. They don't appreciate anything that violates the honored chain-of-command, or that seems unearned. It's important to demonstrate upright motives and good manners at all times. Any use of "bad" language, being late for appointments, sloppy appearance, unwashed cars, talking out of order, and so forth, will count against you. Being polite and respectful could gain you a great ally.

PART TWO: THREE THINGS TO KNOW

Industrious Achievement

In a Hurry to Exploit and Gain Advantage

"YES!!!" IS THE LOUD EXCLAMATION OF VICTORY ACCOMPANIED BY A RAISED fist. This gleeful expression erupts from deep within quite naturally when crossing the finish line in first place (never second), upon surpassing a long-dominant competitor for market share, winning an election, or finally closing the deal on a hard-negotiated contract. This worldview promotes a strong drive to succeed. And success, in this view, is very clearly about material rewards, power, status, and control. The "good life" is equated with a high standard of living—a large material and energy throughput—even though, as noted earlier, this doesn't necessarily correlate with a satisfying life. There exists a common cultural misconception within this worldview that quantitative growth and "more" will result in a qualitatively "better" and more fulfilling life. The fact is often overlooked that an excessively driven, highly competitive lifestyle leaves little room for inner peace.

Nonetheless, this is the competitive industrial-growth mentality that drives the current expansion of the global economy. This is the economic context of most of our early twenty-first century lives. Standing atop (and marketing to) an underlying societal structure of compliant "pedestrian" workers, these achievement-oriented go-getters see and seize endless opportunities for advancement, expansion, and exploitation of resources (human and natural) for "the betterment of society"—and, of course, profit. They have little guilt about unearned privileges. Behind closed doors, they make up their own rules. Individuals with this worldview say what people want to hear, but then do what needs to be done to ensure their own interests. They gladly serve as middle-agents of an oppressive hierarchical economic system, climbing the ladder over and above others, to obtain greater advantage and rewards. This is done, of course, with a polite smile and a warm handshake. They are not necessarily ruthless, however, recognizing that others may be useful in later schemes, and that burning bridges could be bad for repeat business.

They are highly competitive, play to win, and usually do. But their hunger for material prosperity (too often reflecting an inner emptiness) is depleting the Earth's natural resources faster than those resources can regenerate or be recycled. It is a model of industriousness out of control. Yet even as the expansion of global capitalism stalls and teeters on the edge of contraction under the weight of a surging consumer class in developing nations bumping up against the limits of waning finite resources, workers everywhere are pushed to work faster, cheaper and more efficiently. Harried, exhausted, underpaid, and under-supported, many begin to feel that their value as human beings is primarily proportional to their productivity and consumption in the current socio-economic system. The bifurcation of global society into haves and have-nots accelerates. Capital scours the Earth in search of the cheapest labor and natural resources to exploit. The race is on.

This is the current neo-liberal free-market capitalist philosophy in action. This worldview promotes the illusion that unrestrained greed is good for all—that if we all just pursue our own selfish interests as relentlessly as possible and keep the government out of the way (i.e., cut taxes and "starve the beast"), then the "invisible hand" of the market will fill every basket, put a car in every driveway, and result in a rising tide that lifts all boats, not just the yachts of the elite few. To some degree this has been true—depending on where one exists on the socioeconomic scale. But this worldview goes beyond traditional trickle-down rationales. It has led individuals to become heavily invested (psychologically and financially) in the idea of so-called "free trade" (which is not necessarily "Fair Trade") and speculation in the global economy. People with this worldview have no problem with the idea of multinational corporations *über alles*, since they are likely to be among those benefiting as shareholders and consumers. People with this worldview are even in favor of the new "Green" economy, "Conscious Capitalism," or whatever will perpetuate growth and expanding markets.

From a "values and lifestyles" perspective, these are *Individuals* with a capital "I." They don't want or need anyone telling them what to think or how to live—not the government, not religion, not you, nobody. They can see for themselves where the next opportunity lies, and they are surely not going to waste time debating the ethics of whether to jump on it or not. It's a "snooze-you-lose" world. Competitive, privileged, and goal-oriented, their upwardly-mobile aspirations drive them toward ever-greater accomplishment, affluence, and influence. They are results-oriented with a winner-take-all mentality. Progress and change are the way of the world. Technology can solve all problems and will lead the way to a better future for everyone. "Get on board." "Invest early." "The sky is the limit." "You don't want to get caught flat-footed shoeing horses after Henry Ford's arrival." "The next i-gadget is on the way, and it's gonna be *big!*"

At their most admirable, people with this worldview have been pioneering entrepreneurs to whom we are all indebted for whatever conveniences we enjoy. These enterprising individuals are inner-directed and self-actualizing in a way that enables them to look beyond traditional ways of solving problems. Their optimistic risk-taking nature gives them the confidence to both invest in and "sell" their ideas. They rely on hard, rational analysis and scientific method to innovate solutions ahead of the competition. Their energetic focus on results, coupled with sound strategic planning, makes them highly productive and successful. Getting them aligned with the notions of "Natural Capital" and alternative energy could help turn the tide in everyone's favor. They are skilled at spotting a good risk, diplomatically turning down a bad deal, and raising venture capital where a profit can be made.

At its less admirable extreme, this worldview not only tolerates, but encourages, a populace that is materialistic and individualistic to the detriment of the commons. Self-reliance goes beyond short-sighted self-interest to an egotistical (narcissistic) sense of self-importance and entitlement. Individuals might become compulsive and pushy about achieving and having more than everyone else. They may lack conscience or operate in unscrupulous ways where the stakes are high. They justify "collateral damage" as a necessary cost of doing business, and exhibit an elitist, status-conscious attitude that many people ("underlings") find distasteful. Puffed up and acting as self-appointed royalty, they expect others to recognize their specialness and treat them with deference. The cost to those with this worldview is painful loneliness. They use people, and expect that others are using them—that's how life works. They have lots of "contacts," but few real friends. All their power doesn't buy them genuine affection or loyalty. "Let's negotiate a win-win" is the extent of their interest in sharing. They'd be happy to celebrate a mutual victory, but they have a hard time being authentic and intimate because of the vulnerability (weakness) implied. Oh, they might act superficially warm toward those who are currently useful, but their caring is generally based on utility. Getting too close or committed makes them feel trapped. They don't want to need anyone. They want to keep their options open by maintaining a formal distance. But that comfortable distance means they never feel genuinely connected and accepted for who they are as people. Elitism has emotional and interpersonal costs. It's lonely at the top. Fulfillment is not for sale. Dang!

One risk of letting others get too close is being seen for who (they fear) they really are, and then being rejected. Impression management is very important. But behind closed doors, those that know them well know that they can sometimes be very condescendingly critical and contemptuous of people with whom they have just been "warm." Those who are too trusting can end up feeling suckered in, used, and then dumped. The initial calculated appearance of caring and understanding—"I feel your pain"—is effective at extracting information or contacts that might be useful, or as a passing amusement, but when interest or utility wane, people are pretty much treated like yesterday's newspaper—tossed on the pile, out ya go. Any whining about it will only be met with snobbish, disgusted disdain expressed politely as, "It's just business. Business is business, you understand."

In its unhealthy expression, under circumstances where things are *not* going well, individuals with this worldview might become slippery, using "Teflon" tactics (where the evidence never sticks to them), intimidation via emotional dumping, and displacing responsibility to confuse accusers and throw them off the track. They often come out "smelling like a rose" leaving a trail of corpses that can never be linked to them. Their lawyers know how to make "plausible deniability" work in their favor.

The underlying belief manifested by this worldview, regarding humanity's relationship to Earth's natural resources, is primarily utilitarian. Nature should be manipulated with and controlled by technology to create an abundant life for humanity. Nature is here to exploit for a profit, use as a playground, enjoy like a candy store, and serve as a trash can. Suburban sprawl, industrial-chemical agriculture, and technology can and will fix any problems. But this mentality can lead to a sickeningly wasteful extravagance where some people throw out more food at the end of a gala event than many families eat in a month—without any guilt or even recognition of the discrepancy. Pollution and degradation of nature are considered acceptable costs of wasteful conspicuous consumerism. There might even be a profit to be made cleaning it up. But this way of life seems to lead to more and more grandiose displays of opulence—monumental sports arenas, gargantuan shopping malls, the tallest office buildings, and endless road construction for those who can still afford to drive—as an expression of ego-driven competition among elites. Jared Diamond[1] has demonstrated how this type of competitive monument building, which serves the egos of the few, diverts resources away from those infrastructure and societal needs that would better serve the "common" people. Generally, he illustrates with numerous examples, this type of behavior takes place during the last stages of a civilization before its collapse. So much money and energy is spent by the few, competing for dominance among themselves, that the rest of society suffers and eventually falls apart. Game over.

When attempting to dialogue across the divide about these concerns with individuals who are operating from this worldview, it's important to understand that, unless you are a credentialed expert in some area that can help them gain prestige, power, or profit, they are likely to dismiss whatever you have to say as not worthy of consideration. They trust their own observations and conclusions more than yours. And they have already concluded that the current economic model which serves them so well is the best course to pursue—environmentalists be damned.

Unless you have a very impressive, opulent setting in which to entertain (they expect to be treated like VIPs), have a Rolodex of successful elite contacts to share with them, or have some other advantage to enhance their power, status, or image, then you're probably going to be meeting at *their* place, on *their* schedule, and you're going to have to impress them with undeniable scientific data that link environmental concerns to a highly probable financial profit. They might, for example, be convinced by documentation that wind power has tremendous upside growth potential. It helps if the convincing is done with showy marketing materials and wowie-zowie Powerpoint presentations in a short meeting. You might appeal to their competitive nature by demonstrating where the leverage and advantages lie that will lead to success. Ever image-conscious, they don't mind looking like a good person, doing "good works" for society. "Green" is fashionable. They're interested in bigger, better, newer, faster, more powerful, more popular, more efficient, what*ever* the next big thing is—as long as there are good prospects for success. Just make sure you do your homework before the meeting, because they will nail your feet to the floor with penetrating questions that bring visionary ideas down to earth and into their bank account.

Don't overemphasize the "It's good for everybody" theme. Be clear—individuals with this worldview are more interested in entrepreneurial *profits* than a communal "feel good" project. They are interested in rewards for individual performance, not collective happiness. They are above, not one *of*, the masses. They are interested in selling *to* the masses whatever the masses will buy. They expect to be treated as VIPs, not "one of the herd." Keep this in mind when you're communicating or they'll feel slighted and be too busy for further meetings with you. In their minds, they are *not* ordinary and will *not settle* for ordinary, and they don't want *you* to be ordinary. They're only interested in hearing ideas from extraordinary people, and then claiming those ideas as their own. If they feel the idea is their own they're much more interested in the project, and more likely to pursue its implementation. They know how to manipulate the incentives to get people to do what they want, and if others fail to negotiate and bend to their will, they will just go elsewhere and create the conditions necessary for success on their own terms. Don't lose them by being rigid. The future balance of humanity's progress in relation to Earth's natural resources requires their participation.

---

[1] Diamond, J. (2005).

Part One

Why The Book?

The current cultural momentum is:

- unsustainable
- unsatisfying
- conditioned
- fear and greed based
- changeable, but...

- Personal Growth
- Moral Maturity
- Social Evolution
- Human Potential

Part Two

Three Things

Understand the person you are talking with:

- **Section One** their unique CHARACTER STYLE

- **Section Two** their CURRENT WORLDVIEW

- **Section Three** which EXISTENTIAL CONCERN they are struggling with

Part Three

Techniques

You might try:

- listening
- "between the lines"
- parallel their arguments
- question assumptions
- change the context
- stick to common ground
- applaud all steps
- other ideas...

Part Four

Examples

Imagine yourself in:

- An Awkward Event
- A Workplace Conflict
- Air Travel Delay

Section 3) Existential Concerns

A THIRD THING TO KNOW ABOUT THE PERSON TO WHOM YOU ARE TALKING is which source of existential anxiety is most prominent for them at that moment. When talking across the divide about the multiple, converging challenges facing humanity, it is not uncommon for your message to stir up anxiety.

We all have anxiety—deep, inescapable anxiety—resulting from the "givens" of life. Our existence is precarious and fragile. At some level we all know that. Generally, by the time one reaches adulthood, enough disappointment, disillusionment, and suffering has occurred that a sincere questioning of the meaning of it all has arisen. After trying on different identities and belief systems, we conclude that individual responsibility surely plays some role in our destiny. Or does it? Darn if it isn't ever-perplexing. How do synchronicity and chance *really* interact? Or *do* they? I mean, what about Grace? And how can it be that so many people feel so alone on such an over-populated planet? How does *that* make sense? And if we're all going to die anyway, what difference does it make how we live? Oh, why doesn't somebody just figure it all out and tell us? Oh, I forgot. That's the role of religion, or government, or corporate-sponsored media, or ....

The point is that hearing how our civilization is on a collision course with our limited natural resources doesn't exactly soothe the soul. When we talk about "collapse" and "peak oil" and "diminishing resources" we violate the socially collusive layers of denial that allow civilization to bumble along on its cheery way to demise. We stimulate those underlying existential anxieties that throw people's lives into question. This is generally not welcomed and is often met with understandable defensiveness; one's character armor is designed to protect one from anxiety. A rigidification of one's characterological manner of defending against anxiety occurs. People become more like their predictable, characteristic selves under stress, more entrenched in their conditioned ways. They resort to whatever dysfunctional patterns they labor under in a more resolute and desperate way. This does not encourage the transcendence of our neurotic patterns. It doesn't invite reflexive awareness. In fact, it diminishes adaptive intelligence and makes reactive, mechanical functioning more likely. The aggressive become more aggressive. The fearful become more fearful. The compulsive more compulsive, and so forth.

We must consider, however, not just the intensification of a person's individual style of defense against anxiety, but also the interaction between their current *worldview* and whatever specific underlying existential anxiety has been aroused. In this regard, some worldviews encourage dealing with existential anxieties by huddling together and becoming more superstitious, while others seek ruthless individual domination and control when confronted with fearful circumstances. Some strive to adhere to the commandments of a Higher Authority in their search for meaning and order in life. And yet others seek material comfort and prosperity as their path. Different worldviews decipher the same information (about the multiple converging challenges facing civilization) through their particular filters of meaning and beliefs. Each has a specific view and rationale about how the universe works, what the proper roles for humans, nature, economy, and politics are in that universe, and what the purpose and meaning of life really is.

So once again, it's very easy to find ourselves in a situation where we say one thing, and *they* hear another. However, the premise of this book is that, if you listen closely enough to a person's words, you will be able to hear the expression of their unique character style and their current worldview. With this understanding, you can tailor your communications so that your words will have the greatest possible appeal, and will be less likely to offend and cause defensiveness.

If the person's characteristic defenses are skillfully minimized and rendered unnecessary in a "safe" and pleasant dialogue situation, and if enough of the elemental underpinnings of their particular worldview are gently brought into question by new information presented in a palatable manner, then, sometimes that person's character structure might relax enough that they find themselves, and their worldview, temporarily open and malleable enough to consider the possibility of a different vision for making sense of the universe—one that offers stability and hope from another perspective. This is the evolution of consciousness.

Each form of existential anxiety can also be used, in this way, to catalyze a progressive shift in consciousness. For example, awareness of one's mortality after a brush with death can put life into perspective in a way that enhances the fullness of living in the moment. Embracing the inherent lack of structure in life can help cultivate personal responsibility for steering one's life with intelligence and commitment. Realizing one's ultimate aloneness in life illuminates the importance of relationships, community, and a sense of belonging. And the struggle to make sense of it all can encourage us to climb out of apathetic meaninglessness into an engaged, effective life of action.

Let us turn now, to an examination of some commonly shared existential concerns, so that we can have a better and more empathetic understanding of the angst we bring upon ourselves, and others, in our attempts to move society forward.

PART TWO: THREE THINGS TO KNOW

Fear of Death

Denial of Impermanence

THERE'S NO ESCAPING IT. WE MIGHT JOKE ABOUT IT. BUT ULTIMATELY, every one of us struggles with how to accept the imminence of our own death. Bravado fails when the reaper is at the door. A frightful dream fragment, or a loud unexpected sound in the dark—"Boo!"—is usually enough to jolt most of us into an instinctive startle response where our mortality is momentarily upon us.

Anxiety about no longer being alive is an inescapable aspect of life. It's not an easy subject, but let's face it, we have to deal with it. We're going to die, we know that. We just don't know *how* or *when*. We will either exhaust our natural life span (like flashlight batteries growing dimmer and dimmer, then finally out), or experience an untimely death due to accident, illness, and so forth. It is this juxtaposition of *knowing* that death is certain, and the *not* knowing how or when, that results in anxiety. It's also a cause of many interesting, desperate, convoluted twists and turns in our psyches and behavior.

Let's begin by making a distinction between the fear of death and the fear of dying. These are very different fears. Sometimes one is more prominent than the other. Sometimes both besiege us. One is about non-existence. The other is about suffering and indignity. One leaves us up against our actual, ultimate beliefs (whatever we might have proclaimed to the contrary), the other threatens helplessness and humiliation in the face of inescapable pain and pitiful deterioration. The thought of resting at final peace in one's own bed elicits different feelings from images of dying in a horrible accident or in the throes of a slow, agonizing disease process. This is relevant to our topic because, for example, when we talk about things like "environmental degradation leading to the collapse of previous civilizations" or "climate change causing the oceans to rise" we are *more* likely arousing people's fears of *dying* in some sort of Mad Max doomsday calamity scenario, than their fear of "that peaceful final state of rest"—*death*.

Across a communication divide or not, this is a distinction worth paying attention to when talking about such grave matters as the depletion of natural resources. Too often, I observe environmentally aware individuals traumatizing their own compatriots with unnecessarily reactivating language. (Certain individuals within the "peak oil" contingent seem particularly oblivious to this, not unlike the "Left Behind" rapture-scenario proselytizers.) We can just as easily talk about the "contraction" of civilization as the "collapse." In most cases, this still conveys the point. It's generally better, in most circumstances, to leave people in a less panicky state, and therefore better able to consider intelligent options for rational action—both personal and collective—rather than heading for the hills or digging bomb shelters in their backyards.

The point is, most of us don't enjoy, appreciate, or benefit from being reminded, on a regular basis, that we're going to die. It throws a lot of what we're doing up for re-examination. Now, that's not necessarily a bad thing. But it *can* be overdone. The old pop-psychology question—"If you knew you only had six months to live, how would you change your life?"—is valid for those who want to examine the alignment between their behavior and their core values. And I'm all for living in the here-and-now as much as possible. But it's hard to make long-range plans or commitments if you constantly feel up against The End. (Heck, at some point, it stops making sense to buy green bananas.) This, in short, is why we humans employ such a fascinating variety of psychological maneuvers to cope with day-to-day existence in the shadow of death.

Denial, which gets such a bad rap in the world of addiction treatment, is one such defensive maneuver. When it comes to death, denial allows us to carry on with our lives despite the fact that it will all end in loss. Denial is often confused with repression. Repression, generally considered a more admirable defense, is simply the effortless banning of psychological contents from conscious awareness. We will consider, in a moment, how repression is often joined by other useful psychological maneuvers to help us maintain the illusion that death is outside of our self, and that it can be avoided, danced around, or side-stepped gracefully. Denial, on the other hand, tends to be a little more brusque and has more of an "I know it, but don't want to think about it" quality—a sort of defiant, non-acceptance of reality, a refusal to *see*.

One of the more common ways that we tend to use denial to cope with death anxiety is the (mostly subconscious) belief that we are somehow exempt—

"Death doesn't really apply to me." At a very deep level, many (most?) of us believe that somehow, because of our special status in the universe, we will be spared. I know, I know. *You* don't think that. But … it's amazing how many of us actually *do*. Way down deep where nobody, including us, tends to see, there is quite often, as irrational as it might sound, a feeling that somehow we have been chosen, for reasons we don't fully understand, to be spared the fate of all others.

Of course, we don't go around spouting off about this. Heck, most of the time we're not even *aware* of it. In fact, we *deny* it. And we deny that we deny it. It's buried very deep in our subconscious mind. It appears, upon analysis, to stem from early childhood experiences of being watched over and kept from danger by parental caretakers during a "magical thinking" time of development. And it gets reinforced, over the years, by cultural "never grow old" sentiments and religious indoctrinations that espouse an afterlife where one lives on and on. This fits hand-in-hand with another comforting and wishful belief: that there is some supernatural being out there, some larger-than-life parental overseer who has been assigned to watch over us and step in at the crucial moment to rescue us from harm—"Back off reaper, not this one!"

It's easy in one's clear-thinking, awake mind to dismiss this sort of denial as merely childish fantasy or wishful thinking. But it is actually embedded quite deeply in the psyches of most intelligent adults. Believing at a deep unconscious level in our own personal inviolability, and that we have our very own personal rescuer following us around at all times, turns out to be fairly common—even for the non-religious. And the closer the reaper is to the foot of one's bed, the stronger we tend to grasp for this—or anything—that lessens our anxiety. It's quite normal. In the face of death, most people will cling to whatever comforting delusion does the trick, however irrational it might seem in other circumstances. Kubler-Ross[1], in her work on death and dying, helped illuminate the predictable "bargaining" stage of the death process— "Please Lord, give me another chance. I promise to …." Or—"I'll trade you two noisy neighbors and the lazy cat for one more week"—as though death can actually be bargained with. These commonly shared forms of denial, reinforced by cultural myths, form a psychological substratum for fending off the intolerable anxiety that accompanies the realization that death really is quite possible, and is, in fact, inevitable. This primitive denial becomes a foundational basis of character, which is then elaborated and reinforced by layers upon layers of secondary defenses and conditioned patterns of thinking-feeling-behaving, in response to specific life circumstances, resulting in one's unique character style and "script" in life.

Repression, in contrast to denial, is often part of a combined maneuver that allows one to displace the fear *outward* onto an external object or situation. One's life is then dominated by attempts to avoid *that*—the dark, being alone, spiders, snakes, open spaces, other people, public speaking, and so forth. This combination of maneuvers serves to not only disallow the fear of demise from entering one's conscious awareness, but it also, it is hoped, gives one a chance to successfully avoid this external *thing* or *situation*, thus bolstering a sense of safety and control over one's life and fate by acquiring distance from *it* (death). Danger is located "out there" and we can learn to walk around it, or handle it by preparing and fortifying *against* it. This is where we see death anxiety becoming displaced into irrational (phobic and survivalist) behaviors in an attempt to control and dominate nature, situations, and other groups of humans, in order to feel safe.

Another maneuver used to cope with death anxiety, favored mostly by the young and the foolish (not necessarily one-and-the-same), is *challenging* death—gaining a sense of control and mastery over one's destiny by "extreme" or reckless behavior, pushing the limits, and defying death by undertaking dangerous pursuits (e.g., bungee jumping, sky diving, driving dangerously fast, etc.). This is sometimes an unconscious attempt to master feelings of fear and helplessness, to defeat the bogeyman by jeering at him—"Bring it on, Reaper. Catch me if you can." Even seeking out the scariest movies can be used as an attempt to bolster one's courage in the face of terror. This sort of self-reliant stance is not for everyone. But clearly, some individuals are less inclined to look outside of themselves for a "personal savior." They prefer, instead, to look to their own strength, cunning, and fortitude. In their self-estimation, they are tough enough to outwit and outlast the reaper. Rugged and unafraid as it might seem, still, this behavior is often driven by a need to escape anxiety and feelings of helpless about the inevitable. The natural decline of vigor and constitution that comes with age, along with accrued wisdom from the losses and injuries suffered along the way, usually softens this stance over time, eventually resulting in a less bold, more humbled acceptance of an impending end, and the arising of a more spiritual philo-sophical orientation in later years.

It is also true that awareness of our own aging from the relentless passage of time, and recognition that this body-personality-history that we perceive as "I" must inevitably decline and disappear, can serve as an inconvenient reminder to *consciously* move toward a more authentic and meaningfully engaged life. In recognizing that we have, in fact, a limited number of breaths, we begin to take greater interest in understanding our relationship to *this* breath that we are having right now. In this way, facing death not infrequently instigates a welcome shift in perspective for many people. The saying "cancer cures neurosis" illuminates how the sudden inescapable realization that our time is limited thrusts us into awareness that we have not been living fully. A brush with death allows us to see that, even as we age and our physical capacities wane, we are still quite capable of unfolding our human potential in productive and satisfying ways. We may even find that we are happily less hindered by the petty preoccupations of our younger years when we were dulled by illusions of invulnerability. We are finally able to appreciate what is *really* important and may find ourselves becoming more concerned with our legacy beyond the disposition of our accumulated material possessions.

What has it all been about? What have we learned about life, love, courage, and compassion? What have we served? What, in the final analysis, in our pithiest words for posterity, has been true and good and beautiful in this life? How would we have our epitaph read? What might those who come after us learn from *our* struggles, to help them remain mindful along *their own* journey?

It is from such psychological crisis points in our lives, such destabilizing circumstances as adolescence, divorce, death of a significant other, serious injury, the onset of a terminal disease, career disruption, mid-life crisis, and other reversals of fortune that we find an increased ability to focus on what truly matters, setting aside the more trivial concerns in favor of what is essential and true in this very moment. We learn to face life (and death) more fearlessly—but without bravado. Like the turning of a kaleidoscope, we learn to let go, rather than trying to hold on to the previously treasured constellations in our lives. We allow ourselves to be amazed by the continuous unfolding of the endless spectacle. Yes, some "chapters" in our lives have been preferred over others. But in the end, impermanence will have its way; change will prevail whether we try to hold everything still or not. Ka-chink, the kaleido-scope turns, we find ourselves in a new chapter. Coming to grips with this tends to catalyze an awakening of awareness to the non-physical (spiritual) realms of existence which are so easily overlooked in the hurried, harried rush of life: the places where we cling to identities based in the material world —our bodies, our roles, our belongings. Loosening the grip of our anxious attachments to these external factors, we become more curious about that aspect of the self that doesn't change, even as our bodies and minds succumb to the relentless passage of time. Some flee to religious conversion and doctrine out of fear. But for others, facing death can elicit an awareness of the spiritual that is *not* religious. Spiritual in the sense of a non-material—but experienced as real nonetheless—realm of existence which offers meaning and coherence via an unchanging core essence of *being* which is aware, awake, alert, and which feels connected to others and to nature (the web of life) at a "higher" level of consciousness, where we find our identity can *also* rest.

It seems that the degree to which we have lived a meaningful life coincides with the degree to which we are able to face death. At the same time, it seems that the better we are able to embrace our own mortality, the more we are able to live a meaningful life. Paradoxically, the less satisfied we are with our lives, the more anxiety we have about dying—and the more satisfied we are with our lives, the more we are able to face death without panic. We don't want to die having not lived fully. We want to experience and achieve what is important to us before letting it all go.

So the dilemma is a paradoxical given of existence. To face death we must face life. To face life we must face death. In this lies the key to moving beyond our middle-class preoccupations with comfort and security toward a meaningful, engaged life that is truly fulfilling. We must risk moving beyond striving for more and more material accumulation and learn to let go of our culturally reinforced roles in the frenetic, unkind competition for "security," or more accurately, relief from existential anxiety. We must relearn how to move toward and embrace a life that is genuinely healthy and more fulfilling, and perhaps even more "spiritual" in the developmental sense.

That's hard to do in this achievement-oriented society, especially when death is equated with failure and failure with death. It's difficult when our identity is so rigidly cemented to perishable externals in the material realm. But it *is* possible. It's unfortunate that so many of us require a terminal diagnosis before awakening to the idea that existence cannot be postponed. It's sad that so many wait until the last few months of their lives to really live. Missed opportunities are just that. This is it! There's no going back. Life continues to unfold in the present moment as a series of *nows*—now, now, now. Wasting *this* precious moment worrying or regretting only takes time away from focusing on and enjoying those people, those activities, those experiences that offer the depth, truth, and meaning that we long for *right now*. Learning to embrace what *is*, to count our blessings, to savor and be grateful for whatever we can muster the presence for, can become a "practice" that helps us overcome death anxiety without all of the detrimental dramatic elaborations attempting to stave off the inevitable. It can help us to stop destroying nature and each other in futile attempts to ward off what we must ultimately embrace with wisdom and compassion.

So, when we talk among ourselves, or across a divide about issues that stimulate this unbearable anxiety about the fragility of life, let's strive to have a little more awareness and compassion—for ourselves and for others. Because, when we trigger each other's survival anxiety, it's only going to be defended against in ways that are probably *not* going to result in good communication or rational action—both of which we need more of as we seek to collectively, consciously evolve toward a sustainable and just global community.

---

[1] Kubler-Ross, E. (1969).

PART TWO: THREE THINGS TO KNOW

Uncomfortable with Uncertainty

Lack of Structure and Implied Responsibility

"WE LIVE IN UNCERTAIN TIMES" IS A CLICHÉ TOO OFTEN USED BY THE POWER-HUNGRY politicians of empire seeking to garner agreement for oppressive policies. The truth is, humanity has *always* lived in uncertain times. Uncertainty is one of those "givens of existence" that humanity has *always* been uncomfortable with, and has gone to great lengths to try to avoid, deny, and assert control over.

There is actually a constellation of factors intertwined here: the fact that there is no structure or set of guidelines to follow in life except what we fabricate or accept from the assertions of others; the fact that the physical universe in which we live, and are a part of, is continually shifting and changing (evolving), which makes it impossible to find anything solid to hang on to; the both welcomed and dreaded reality of self-determination in life (that it is up to *us* to choose which direction to step in at every moment); and the inescapable fact that we must bear responsibility for the consequences of our every choice —individually and collectively.

We really *can* change the structure in our lives, if we are unhappy with it. We really *can* choose to head down a different path, as a society, if we want to. Acknowledging the alarmingly large array of options before us, coupled with the freedom to steer our course, however, results in a nearly unbearable degree of anxiety about our responsibility for how things turn out. We also find that to the degree we "fail" (in our own eyes, and in the eyes of societal expectations) to manifest our fullest human potential in this one-and-only life that we know about for sure, we experience guilt, self-depreciation, and despair. Also disturbing, as we are busily charting our own course, is the realization that life is ultimately indifferent. If we make poor choices that lead to suffering—we suffer. Life doesn't really care. If we fall off a ladder— "Boom!"—we hit the ground. Period. This insults our sense of "specialness" in the universe, and contradicts the comforting delusion that life (or some unseen personal protector) is looking out for us.

Let's try teasing these different strands apart and examining them separately, although it must be understood that they operate holistically in our everyday experience. Why? Because these are some of the difficult feelings that get restimulated and defended against in characteristic (characterological) ways when we talk about the "changes" that are upon us as a civilization.

To begin, let's acknowledge that life has no inherent structure that must be adhered to, and that this is both welcomed and a source of angst. On the one hand, we enjoy the freedom and like the idea of self-determination in life. But with it comes anxiety about the ultimate responsibility implied for how things turn out. Every little choice we make sets us in a direction where one thing must be chosen over another, and it's not always easy to know, beforehand, what will be the best choice in the end. As we grow more emotionally mature, we learn that we must accept responsibility either way. We realize that we cannot continue to blame others, blame "the system," or fate, or God, or even *ourselves* for poor choices. Because ultimately, it's not about blame. It's about responsibly steering our course toward a future of our choosing, not beating ourselves up over past mistakes. We learn to take hold of life's steering wheel because we must, ultimately, live with the consequences of our choices. The consequences do have an effect on us and our life. It is our life, and the universe really *doesn't* care if our choices are beneficial or self-defeating. To use the ladder analogy again, if we fall off a ladder, gravity has its way with us. Period. This is *not* to deny that there are sometimes (often?) contextual forces beyond our immediate awareness or sense of control that, ideally, would be factored in when making a decision. But generally, if we admit it, we do have *some* measure of control over whether we get on the ladder or not, how we set the ladder up, and whether we pay attention to being safe while we're on the ladder. Thus we bear *some* responsibility for the outcome.

It would seem that those who are more inclined to accept personal responsibility, where it is reasonable and possible, are often more frustrated with those external contextual forces that seem beyond their control, such as cultural institutions that perpetuate inequality, climate change, peak oil, and so forth. Running up against such seemingly intransigent external factors can result in a sense of dismay and feeling unfairly thwarted. Aspirations for social change can sometimes deflate when it feels like "The more you take responsibility, the more you suffer."

On the other hand, those who tend to believe that responsibility for life events lies *beyond* their control (e.g., fate, God, the market, etc.) sometimes seem to be more susceptible (i.e., suggestible) to manipulation by targeted corporate-sponsored media campaigns, charismatic politicians, fundamentalist religious leaders, and so forth. Such individuals (research has shown) also tend to live with greater feelings of powerlessness, hopelessness, anxiety, and confusion, as well as being less politically active. Their "learned helplessness" is, in some measure, a function of this externalization of responsibility. They believe that they are helpless to change their circumstances.

All of this is completely understandable. We wish it were different. We are all desperate for something steady to hold onto, something solid to stand on, some firm ground under our feet. But, disappointingly, life is ultimately groundless—constantly shifting sands. The culturally prescribed structures just don't seem to be working for an increasing number of people on many different levels. Guilt kicks in—"What's wrong with me? Why am I not content just watching TV and shopping at the mall like everybody else?" The options offered by the current socio-economic system are a misfit for our human needs. But letting go and stepping into what feels like a great, structureless void arouses such anxiety from the uncertainty about what sort of future our choices might lead to, that many (most?) yield to that fear and eagerly accept a role, a niche, in the hierarchy of exploitation and upwardly-flowing profits, in order to escape the pain.

When we talk with people about the oncoming convergence of challenges that will likely result in a re-organization of how we live as a global civilization, we are triggering this anxiety about an uncertain future, without giving them anything to hang on to. This is why it is comforting to use concepts that begin to make sense of what's happening—big ideas that embrace the larger patterns of change that we are all experiencing. For example, "Sustainability," "Conscious Evolution," "Permaculture," and "The Great Turning" are concepts that tend to capture the progressive imagination and help people to embrace a lot of uncertainty within a context of meaning that lessens their anxiety. The idea of being part of an "emerging culture" that feels better than our current life, is more easily welcomed and embraced than descriptions of collapse and chaos followed by who knows what. This is important, especially when we are asking people to stand for convictions that are not supported by authority and that go against the pop-culture consumer trance. This is where we feel *really* alone and afraid and in need of support and validation for dissenting views. Under *these* circumstances, it's too tempting to avoid responsibility, to subordinate our autonomy and embrace authoritarianism, in order to feel safe. Exercising our freedom to choose, in life, is not always comfortable.

But we do have to choose. And we do have some freedom to choose. We are free to choose among options and decide which way we will go. We are free to choose how we will spend our time and money, and where we will place our attention. In this regard, we are "creating" our own life, and collectively co-creating our civilization. We do have some power to make things the way we want them. And, it's an ongoing process. We don't just choose once, and then we're done. We are faced with ever-changing circumstances, and we must continually choose and act and adapt. As we become more aware, we begin to recognize and accept, that every choice has implications beyond our own personal well-being. Every act of will has social and political implications. Even the paralysis of procrastination is revealed as decisive in many situations, as we are held accountable for our failures to act, as well as our actions—"I should have secured the ladder before getting on it." Or— "I should have spoken up when they were taking the Jews."

Asserting our will, in life, is how we move from wishing to doing. It's true that non-doing can also be an expression of one's will, as for example, *not* eating meat, *not* participating in the exploitation of others, *not* voting, and so forth. But generally, asserting our will is how we bring our vision of the future into manifestation. We *will* the future we want to live in and, to some degree, we are continually trying to influence others to will that *same* future as *we* desire—in this case, a more sustainable and equitable society. Welcome to politics. However, in our engagement of community, in this co-creating of a future that is based on our best combined intelligence, we must be ever-on-guard against getting snagged into a "contest of wills" where defensiveness and divisiveness pull us away from our interdependence with each other and the synergy of our collective wisdom. On the other hand, willfulness, in the sense of resisting having one's destiny controlled by others without any say in the matter, should not be seen as negative, but rather as an act of self-determination in life where one is taking a passionate stance *for* something. (see the FOR words section on page 35) As Tom Atlee points out,

134

"Being against something does not bring what one wants into being." What are you *for*?

As we move from wishing to willing, we confront choice. We must decide which way to proceed. And deciding is often a lonely act. No one can decide for us. We must choose one among several competing wishes. This is usually accompanied by some measure of conflict and anxiety. The more equivalent the two sides of the choice are, the harder it is to make a decision. And, for time-limited opportunities (which *all* are, really, in the final analysis), we cannot hide behind indecision. The passage of time will decide for us. Important decisions are difficult, also, because they make us confront how alone we really are, how short life really is, how responsible we ultimately are, and how guilty we will feel if we waste our one shot at the life we really wanted. Each decision denounces some possibility, and thus limits our parameters as we continue to move inexorably closer to death. It takes courage to choose (and renounce) with awareness in our attempt to live life well, with as few regrets as possible at the end.

Sometimes we need to go slowly, to consider our options carefully, and to take enough time for things to settle and clarify before we choose among alternatives that seem very equal. Sometimes we procrastinate and let the decision be made for us—"Now that oil is getting harder to come by, I guess we'll *have* to drive less." Or, we deny reality—"Global warming isn't gonna kill us, it'll just be more like summer all the time." Or, we seek escape— "Let's go to the mall and do some shopping." Or, "zone out" in front of the TV—"Let's see what's on." We can be quick to delegate responsibility—"It's God's will that we use up all of the natural resources in our lifetime. Besides, the President said that we should keep shopping." And then, after the decision has been made for us, we devalue the unchosen alternative to lessen our post-decisional regret—"What's so good about *old* trees, anyway? I kinda like the way those young monoculture forests look like a golf course."

It's so much easier, as an "outsider" (e.g., as a parent, a friend, a therapist, etc.), to see when other people are making choices that are likely to lead to suffering, than when we are the ones making a "dumb move." Our inclination, with others, is to remind them that they have a choice. We see, in these moments, how clearly the course of our lives is the result of the hundreds of little choices that we make every day and the correlated actions that stem from them.

It's so much easier to see in others than when it's *our* tough decision, or *our* habitual pattern and stubborn resistance that is driving a decision. As we gain more insight, we also begin to realize that some decisions are truly "fateful" and will have ramifications many years from now—"Maybe suburban sprawl wasn't such a good layout for human habitation after all." Maturity and learning (the result of impulsive action leading to suffering) might eventually lead us to take a little more time with *big* decisions—to feel more deeply and think more clearly, or to ask for advice from trusted others before making a final decision.

Even so, accepting responsibility remains our challenge. Especially with "difficult" decisions—the ones that make us so acutely aware of the fundamental groundlessness of life, where the path forward is truly unclear and we *must* choose. We (humans) have adopted a variety of maneuvers to try to slip away from such responsibility. As mentioned before, we'd really like someone else to make the tough decisions for us, and then reassure us that everything will turn out all right. Unfortunately this is not possible, although many charlatans and religious and political leaders might quickly step up to say that they can. Under duress, many people are more likely to compliantly follow "assurances" of security by "authority" and accept whatever structure and diversions are offered to help them escape the discomfort of having to think for themselves and accept responsibility for difficult choices. Obviously, this can result in a rigid, non-thinking populace that is easily manipulated for profit. Ultimately, we must all learn to manage our own lives. And, it is the collective managing of our individual lives that gives rise to the structures of civilization. There is a reciprocal determination happening here. We affect civilization and civilization affects us. This is important. There is power for change in this equation!

When we talk about the coming changes due to the playing out of the multiple converging challenges facing humanity in the decades ahead, we need to recognize that it shakes the assumptive state of most people's lives, and makes apparent that all such assumed structures of existence (social, political, economic, etc.) are, in fact, arbitrary and subject to continual change. Some say, "Hoorah! Let it fall." Others tremble and huddle together in fear. These different reactions are partly due, as we've seen, to whether people experience responsibility and control in life as lying *within* themselves, or whether responsibility and control are attributed to some *external* factor (e.g., fate, God, the market, etc.).

Generally speaking, those who have been raised in more consistently warm and responsive early-life circumstances tend to feel more empowered about the possibilities of asserting their will in life, and affecting change for the better. Others, who suffered more unpredictable and unfriendly early lives, tend to feel more helpless and look externally for structure and certainty. These latter individuals are more likely to favor political leaders, religions, bosses, mates, and so forth, who project a strong sense of certainty and provide a lot of structure. Such individuals don't feel equipped with enough internalized confidence and strength to face the reality of their existential situation and manage, successfully, the feelings of uncertainty and its accom-panying anxiety.

This should give us some clue as to how we might interact in a way that will probably be the most helpful and well received by those who feel the most disempowered and vulnerable about their role in co-creating a better future. An accepting and validating presence makes it easier for people to listen, think, and change. Admonishing unsustainable behavior or detrimental internalized cultural values will likely only arouse guilt, and replicate early hurtful, invalidating situations they grew up in, calling forth inevitable defensiveness. Perhaps one goal of talking across the divide would be to help such individuals reconsider their belief that help must necessarily come from a source *outside* of themselves, i.e., that it is possible to assume personal and collective responsibility for the transformation of society (within reason). I say "within reason" because, as we've seen, the arousal of guilt can be counter-productive. Ultimately, we *are* responsible, as society arises from our collective decisions. But it doesn't help to stimulate guilt if we can avoid doing so.

A useful distinction might be made, at this point, between existential guilt and neurotic guilt. While the subjective *experience* at a physiological level might be quite similar, the genesis and implications differ widely. Both are unpleasant and yet both have some merit. Regular "garden variety" neurotic guilt is usually the result of some minor (real or imagined) transgression. This type of guilt can be a good thing, to the extent that it helps us to be more "civilized" and considerate of each other—"I shouldn't have said that so harshly." Existential guilt, on the other hand, stems from a sense of not living up to our full potential in life. And *this* can be useful for motivating us toward greater authenticity and self-actualization. No one wants to end up on their death bed saying, "I really should have done such-and-so with my life while I had the chance." While I had the chance. There it is. We *always* have the chance. We are *always* in the process of "becoming"—ever-growing, ever-changing, ever-choosing, and continually evolving. Overcoming the anxiety of uncertainty and stepping beyond existential guilt requires taking an "I can" stance. We must act with courage to bring our highest vision into reality or suffer the regret and guilt over not living our life to our fullest.

We must acknowledge that only "we" can change the life we have created, and that the responsibility for choosing, deciding, and acting in accordance with our deepest held convictions and values is continuous and ongoing. This is empowering—"To get what I really want, I must choose among the considered possibilities, decide on one, develop a plan, and act effectively." To do otherwise is to yield to feelings of powerlessness and to shirk responsibility for one's life. We don't need to wait for permission. We don't need to spend our time-limited lives trying to fulfill irrational cultural expectations. We need not waste time delving into guilt over past mistakes. It's better to use that guilt about not fulfilling our destiny as motivation to decide and act in ways that are more closely aligned with our unique, authentic selves and our vision for a better world. This is accepting responsibility for one's life.

We feel existential guilt to the degree that we fail to fulfill authentic possibility in our lives. And because no one is perfect or completely self-actualizing and congruent, and because our potential is unlimited in some capacities, guilt about our unlived potential is yet another one of those givens of existence that we cannot escape without resorting to maladaptive maneuvers. Using existential guilt for motivation, instead of as an excuse for despair and self-recrimination, makes all the difference in whether we approach life from an empowered and effective place, or a listless, passive, cynical, resigned place. Yes, there are compromises to be made in order to "pay the rent" in this current socio-economic system. And yes, it is not always easy. It is, in fact, more difficult the closer one is to dealing with those basic survival and safety needs at the "lower" end of the socio-economic scale. But what is also true is that accepting responsibility for one's life means accepting, by implication, the failures and limitations of the current system, and the global train wreck that lies ahead—"If only we had taken global warming and peak oil more seriously sooner, our children wouldn't suffer so."

To the degree that we realize and admit that we have condoned with our silence, and participated through our compliance and passivity, in the co-creation of global circumstances that teeter on the edge of dissolution (with a high probability of unprecedented massive human suffering), we experience appropriate guilt. Our collective, short-sighted greed, indifference, and denial may also undo many of our beloved cultural achievements, resulting in a less desirable future for our children and grandchildren many generations forth. To change our course will require us all to acknowledge our collusion in the atrocities we have personally and collectively gone along with, and to bear the associated guilt in healthy and productive ways.

It's asking a lot to ask people to stop unthinkingly accepting the rules and "mandates" that have been handed to them, to think carefully and critically about the implications of their choices and their continued participation in a culture run amok, to think about and question with their own minds, and to discuss among their friends and neighbors the validity (or invalidity) of the assumptions upon which our global society currently operates. It's asking a lot, and it's not easy. But it *is* possible, and we *can* do it.

PART TWO: THREE THINGS TO KNOW

Mired in a Meaningless Life

What's It All About?

"So, let's see if I've got this straight. We're floating around in a big empty universe that really doesn't care, one way or the other, what happens to us. And, after wandering around in our self-created hell for a few decades, we're just gonna die anyway. Okay, so, tell me again ... what's the point?" The point is ... there is no point.

Painfully, the existentialists have already laid us bare about the absurdity and meaninglessness of it all. Yet humanity's search for meaning continues unabated. The incessant gnawing leads us to all sorts of maladaptive maneuvers in our attempt to escape the underlying feelings of pointlessness, insignificance, and hopelessness about what life has to offer. People turn to drugs and alcohol, TV, computer games, religion, sports mania, consumerism, activism, escapist travel, dangerous thrill seeking, and other such distractions, in their desperation to find something that makes life worth living—something that gives life a sense of purpose. We seem to have an inherent need to have something worthwhile to aim for and struggle toward. Without a goal or direction inspiring us to strive, we tend to deflate and feel that we are drifting aimlessly.

There is, of course, no one answer to the question of what gives life meaning —no single, universal way to achieve a sense that one's place in the universe is the right one. It is something that each individual sojourner through existence must discover and embrace for themselves.

Setting aside the obvious grasping for meaning via doctrinal "truths" espoused by the myriad religions of the world, many turn to activities which tend to be either *self*-oriented (e.g., self-indulgence, self-enhancement, self-expression), or activities that reach beyond the personal self toward some vision of a better life, (e.g., a higher purpose, a greater good.) This latter approach often takes the form of altruistic dedication to some cause or campaign that one believes will make life better for everyone.

It is true that *all* of these activities, whether self-oriented or altruistic, have merit in that they offer relief from the nagging sense of being lost in "the great void," and should be recognized as having benefit and value for *that*, if nothing else. But it is also true, as we shall see, that those who remain wedded to self-oriented activities—even though they are often undertaken with good intent, as forms of personal healing and attempts to cope with the pain of existence—sometimes remain "stuck" in isolated lives that revolve around the correlated symptoms of meaninglessness without ever directly addressing the underlying concern.

Materialism has its place in the sense that it can uplift one's spirits by improving one's living conditions. The problem is, in affluent societies it has been taken to such an exaggerated, grotesque, and ultimately ineffective extreme by this profit-driven culture of ours that it no longer delivers meaning. Likewise, hedonistic indulgence, which could be about living life fully and enjoying pleasure for its own sake, has been taken beyond any sense of awe for how amazing life is, and too easily becomes a culturally-reinforced addiction that weakens moral character and promotes indifference toward the larger ramifications of our actions (namely, the suffering of exploited others and depletion of natural resources). The short-lived relief attained by getting and having material *things* is highly addictive. And the belief that our life will be better as a result is really just an illusion of the cultural trance. In fact, this coping strategy more commonly leads to a lot of unsatisfying, irrational, compulsively-driven, frenzied activity in an attempt to achieve some particular internal feeling-state via externalities. The all-too-common result is physical, emotional, and spiritual exhaustion, which is actually a form of relief in itself, in that one is too tired to continue striving and *must* stop. This is one of the reinforcing factors that *strengthens* the consumer addiction, not unlike the post-orgasm collapse that reinforces compulsive sexuality by temporarily flattening the anxiety that drives it.

Unless one's circumstances are truly dire, in which case attending to basic physical and security needs with such intense purpose would be appropriate and necessary, then spending one's time and life-energy focused on amassing material objects and wealth in an attempt to gain some sense of mastery over meaninglessness in life is ultimately futile. Sooner or later this strategy will fail and leave one depleted, dismayed, and generally very alone. Not a good state to find oneself in when confronting the existential void. This, unfortunately, is too often the situation faced by those whose lives have been spent seeking power, prestige, and prosperity via materialism and hedonistic self-indulgence. When faced with a consequential reversal of fortune (as happens in many lives) such as the loss of a loved one, a financial downturn, terminal diagnosis, or (appropriate to our discussion) sudden comprehension of the implications of peak oil, such individuals may find themselves thrown into an existential crisis.

Sometimes a life-disrupting event is needed for such externally focused individuals to discover the inward journey. It is often after such a wake-up call that self-discovery, personal growth, and striving to fulfill one's unique potential arises as a source of meaning and purpose. We suddenly become aware that we have been "efforting" in the wrong direction. We become acutely aware that we have a unique set of feelings, talents, motivations, interests, viewpoints, and so forth. "How fascinating," we think. Self-absorption in getting to know the authentic self becomes a quest worthy of a lifetime. We become aware of how we have been socialized into accepting ill-suited goals and roles that have impinged on our fragile inner self, which has been trying to unfold along its *own* idiosyncratic trajectory. One tires of being squashed by conventionality and affirms a new stance in life—"I am unique, and I have my *own* life to live."

The risk here, of course, is of getting stuck in one's own process, in one's "specialness," in an overbalanced way that excludes the social and environmental context. Sometimes, early into the healing process, this mindset that "It's all about me" is necessary for shutting out the confusing cultural expectations and the influences of well-meaning others so that we can "find our self." We retreat from the world and regroup. But then, at some point, we must reemerge and take a stand and share with the world what we have learned.

In this way, self-discovery eventually leads to an interest in self-expression—"I am unique and valuable. Therefore, my personal expressions are unique and valuable." Creative[1] pursuits take on new meaning. We are captivated by our own ability to create authentic expressions of our uniqueness. And while still very much self-involved and inward-focused, creativity, it turns out, can be a valuable companion for renewal and integration along the continually unfolding path toward meaning. Creative self-expression is justified, at first, as having value in itself. The act of creation is good and true and meaningful. And if the message has social value, so much the better, but "create I must." Over time, we discover that creativity has become the cultivation of courage —the willingness to explore and try new solutions to complex problems. Creativity becomes internalized as a way of *being* in the world—a way that is less afraid and more boldly willing to address the empty canvas of life in this very moment, from a deep, trusting sense of one's capability of generating satisfactory solutions—authenticity and generativity combined. This grounding in our essential nature as "creative life force" manifesting with awareness in so many individual ways, is what is now being required of us, collectively, in order to move forward into a truly sustainable, compassionate future together as a global community.

This next step, however, toward collective co-creation, will require us to move beyond our individual involvement with creative acts. In order to experience a true and more substantial sense of meaning and purpose in life, one must ultimately step across the line from self-interest into self-transcendence. One must reach for something outside the individual self, for something greater than oneself. There must be some higher purpose. The personal self must be honored and included, but also surpassed. Self-understanding provides the platform on which one must stand in order to reach even higher. Otherwise, to remain preoccupied with "healing" (or grieving, or guilt, or self-expression) can become just another form of self-centered behavior that fails to deliver true meaning and a sense of purpose. There is a point of diminishing returns. We are all capable of knowing where that point is for us as individuals— the point where the more we focus on the self, the less satisfying we find it. This is as it should be. Moral maturity correlates with an expanded range of concern—caring for others we know and love, caring for others we will never know, caring for a future we will not live to enjoy. Civilization thrives when elders plant trees.

It is here that altruism, in the truest sense, reveals its value. Putting aside arguments that altruism might be ultimately self-serving, it behooves us to consider how the desire to leave the world a better place, by doing what we are capable of, can be part of a natural progression in regaining a sense of power and meaning in life. Committing our self to a direction or cause that gives us a chance to contribute to something more important than our own individual life calls forth our greatest efforts. We are lifted out of our conditioned fears and timidity. We feel inspired by our connection to a vaster scope of possibility. We transcend the limited, individual self and feel connected to something much greater and more significant. We feel engaged and alive in a way that breaks us free of the deadening weight of cultural apathy and cynicism. At these times, there is clarity and coherence in our vision. Our aims become more obvious. No longer dysphoric about the apparent paradoxes of a screwed-up world, we transcend helplessness and experience increased efficacy without a sense of urgency. We no longer need some culturally ordained version of what life should be about. We experience the creative unfolding of life, and our role in it, moment by moment. Meaning is discovered and experienced simply by staying connected, in the present moment, to that unfolding of our higher purpose with courage and fascination. Compassion for the suffering and oppression found all around us, moves us beyond our preoccupations with comfort and security, and provides plenty to live for. Engagement in action that manifests our caring doesn't eliminate the meaninglessness of life so much as it causes it to not matter as much. It is intrinsically rewarding to involve ourselves in caring about people and projects, and to build toward a future we believe in. Whether it is true or not, it does us well to act as if it is, because at the very least, it brings us meaning and purpose and pleasure. Engagement is an antidote to meaninglessness. Our lives are no longer plagued by the "luxury" of searching for meaning, nor organized around such seemingly insignificant goals as personal indulgence or the acquiring of material objects. We take pleasure and meaning in generating creative solutions to seemingly perplexing problems—with ease and enjoyment. A new passion and purpose has been discovered.

The transcendence of conditioned, cultural inhibitions and confusions is not only possible, but, at this juncture in our collective evolution as a species, *necessary*, in order to bring into existence the world we all ultimately want to live in. The old values and structures lose our interest (and participation) as they crumble and fade away. Meanwhile, the possibilities for co-creating an emerging culture of cooperative abundance continue to become more vivid.

When we find ourselves talking across the divide about the magnitude of required change that is upon us, we should keep in mind that grasping for some sense of meaning, some sense of coherence, some way to make sense of all that is happening in the world around us, is getting "triggered" (and defended against) by our conversation.

We are often, without intending to, stimulating other people's awareness of the utter lack, or tenuous construction, of meaning and purpose in their lives—of how shallow and ineffective their coping strategies really are. This doesn't feel good. Especially if the individual is prone to depressive low self-esteem, or has difficulty finding and hanging on to their authentic self. For these individuals, what *we* might feel is a reasonable conversation about valid concerns, might be experienced by *them* as reactivation of deep shame and fear and feelings of being utterly lost about how to find something worth living for. It tosses them, unprepared, into "the void" and sends them scrambling for old escapist coping mechanisms, some of which may be quite self-defeating, for example, alcoholism, obsessive-compulsive busy-ness, frantic consumerism, submitting and conforming to unhealthy cultural expectations, and so forth. Even charging from one successful social/political campaign to the next can be an activist's version of the struggle to find meaning. This doesn't mean that enthusiasm for social change isn't good or helpful, but we need to recognize that *any* activity can be used as a defense against the intolerable feelings of meaninglessness and insignificance.

In general, action overcomes apathy. To frustrate anyone's grasp for meaning is unnecessary, unkind, and unhelpful. Don't go there. The existentialists, as was pointed out earlier, have already played that out. And while it makes for interesting philosophy, it doesn't do much to move things forward in a positive direction. Avoid the temptation to point out how futile someone's attempts to find meaning seem. We are all capable of discovering the path forward for ourselves, given enough support and empathy. Rest assured, just talking calmly about all of the changes that are upon us as a civilization is more than enough stimulation to reactivate predictable defensive maneuvers in our attempts to cope with the underlying "So then, what's the point?" feelings.

As always, it's important to keep in mind that different people are likely to be affected differently. In general, individuals who tend toward introversion and low self-esteem are likely to also struggle with finding meaning in their lives. To the dismay of some progressive liberals, with regard to finding a sense of purpose and engagement in life, there is a case to be made for the role of religion in people's lives. Those who confidently espouse strong religious

146

beliefs and conservative values tend to experience less difficulty with purpose and meaning. Sometimes that rigid, puritan arrogance that seems so unexamined and drives many liberals nuts can actually be useful by providing a sense of belonging to a group, a cause, a transcendent worldview, and a set of guidelines that result in relief from existential anxiety about the meaninglessness of life. Whether or not it's congruent with a deeper sense of authenticity is not the question here. For many, it might be a *stage* in their evolution of consciousness. What gives meaning in life continues to change over time. But it seems to always require some fit between one's goals, one's roles, and one's values. And whether those are adopted from outside oneself, or discovered through painstaking self-analysis, an adaptive adjustment is sought and it tends to last as long as it is not disrupted—as long as one feels that progress is being made in the "right" direction.

So, when talking across the divide, we must be careful to not offend another person's adaptive stance with regard to meaning in their life. It may, in fact, be working quite well for them. I mean, come on. How well is *yours* working? It's not that easy for an outside observer to understand, at a glance, all of the implications, on an internal psychological level, that may be involved in what sounds like a not-very-well-thought-through position. Listen. Listen closely. And you may hear something useful for your own ever-incomplete search for meaning. This is where the "co" in co-created future enters.

The real point is that we're trying to help each other recognize that the way we've got things set up, as a civilization, is not as good as it could be. What we want to do is find a way to invite people to participate in the "Great Turning" or "Conscious Evolution" or however *you* say it (and they can hear it)—realizing everyone's potential for higher functioning as a global community. War is *not* inevitable. Exploitation and oppression are *not* inevitable. Greed is *not* inevitable. We can transcend those impulses, together, and be among those who lead the way to a collective awakening of humanity into a new era. We don't need to cling to the old, self-defeating ways that once provided a sense of security and meaning in the big, empty universe. We can create new, more intelligent ways of living our shared lives on this one planet. We can continue to learn and refine our values and policies so that they provide useful guidelines for action that take us in directions that we actually want to proceed as a society. We *can* engage in lives that feel as if they matter and that *do* make a significant, positive difference. Yes, we will die anyway. But that doesn't mean that nothing is important.

We must help each other to see that "meaning" is an individual and a relative thing. This is not easy because it's all so unclear and so we tend to avoid conversations that roam into this area. Yet our desire to communicate across the divide inevitably reactivates this baffling existential concern. We can see, perhaps more easily, where someone is veering off into escapist indulgences or the pursuit of material aggrandizement in their attempts to cope. But it gets tricky when we try to point out how self-absorption can actually thwart a deeper sense of meaning that might be found outside the self. And it gets even more complicated when we bump into rigidly held belief structures and values that seem, quite evidently to the holder of such beliefs, to be working better than our *own* ill-defined conceptions. Hmmm.

We must learn to be curious about each other and express concern for our shared vulnerabilities. None of us want to see our children and grandchildren live in a world that is less wonderful than the one we inherited. Connecting around these sorts of issues helps us *all* to feel connected to and in agreement about a larger, transcendent vision worth working toward together. What *can* be done, with the establishment of enough trust and caring in our relationships, is to nudge our way toward an understanding of the possible inconsistencies in the person's stance between their values, their assumptions, their beliefs, and their behavior. In talking across the divide we need to help people get unstuck from their apathy and hopelessness about finding meaning in life, in an authentic way. Encourage them to talk about how they have given up their hopes and their vision of a better society. Help them explore the ways in which they have settled for a life that denies their self-transcendent aspirations. Help them unravel the inconsistencies of their logic and overcome those inhibitions that keep them feeling and playing small in life.

If the person you are talking to says that, "Ultimately nothing matters, and since nothing matters, there is no point to trying." You might try countering with something like, "Well, if nothing really matters, then it shouldn't matter that nothing matters." (Apparently it matters to them that it doesn't matter.) Besides, even if nothing matters, that doesn't necessarily mean that we have to feel angst about it. We could just as well feel entertained by the comical irony and absurdity of it. It's only when we are in the grips of a gloomy perspective that we feel, "Oh my God, there is no point to living." Fortunately, that is only one viewpoint and it is active only part of the time we spend here on earth. Other times, we feel differently and things *do* seem to matter simply because they *matter*. Meaning is not a prerequisite of mattering. Also, just because something that used to matter no longer matters at this moment, doesn't mean that it *didn't* matter when it did, or that it was a waste of time when it *did* provide meaning.

At a very basic human level, we're all trying our best to figure out how to love, be loved, and move forward together toward a future that represents our highest commonly held values and wishes. And if *this* isn't the point ... somebody please tell me what is.

---

[1] It's important to keep in mind that creativity doesn't necessarily mean Fine Arts. It can be a garden, a recipe, a conversation, or whatever. It is the mindful attention to expression of authentic creative intelligence that matters. The point is *how* it was undertaken and whether one found challenge and meaning in stretching beyond one's normal conditioned patterns to create something new and different and better as an expression of one's truth. Did it make things better or more beautiful for others? Or was it just another masturbatory cathartic escape from feeling lost and aimless in a culture in which one can't seem to find a niche.

All Alone in the Universe

Separation and Isolation versus Connection and Belonging

SEPARATION IS AN ILLUSION. THIS SEEMS TO BE THE CONSENSUS AMONG systems theorists, quantum physicists, permaculture designers, Buddhist scholars, Bioneers, and others. All of life is connected. We humans are but one manifestation of that interconnected vibrational life force that *is* the universe. What we experience as the world of sensory phenomena around us is really just a very narrow, limited-frequency span of the totality. The universe is a boundless ocean of energetic potential. Our experienced existence is a conscious part of it. We are all connected. More and more of us recognize that fact.

"Yeah, so what?" you say.

"If we're all so connected, then why the heck do I feel so darn alone!?"

We'll need to begin by making a distinction between loneliness and aloneness. One is a feeling, the other a life circumstance. After that, we can begin to understand how both the influence of society and the process of human emotional maturation contribute to our experience. After examining some of the ways we try to wiggle out of our discomfort about how ultimately alone we are in the universe, we'll explore what this means in terms of talking across the divides in our everyday lives about the challenges we face as a civilization. We'll also look at how we might move from feeling so separate and isolated, to feeling more connected with others and enjoying a true sense of belonging and community.

All right then. Consider that being alone is *not* the same as being lonely. We know this, but the two so often go together, that it's easy to forget and mix them up in our minds. What most people experience as *loneliness* is usually the result of feeling separated, on an interpersonal level, from other human beings. Sometimes this is the result of an individual's characteristic ways of relating that make interpersonal closeness problematic. For example, some individuals may find themselves socially isolated because their interpersonal style is so difficult for others to be around, such as a person who is overly aggressive, too frequently invalidating, excessively narcissistic, or distressingly manipulative. On the other end of the spectrum, some people are so extremely shy and conflicted about interpersonal contact that they fail to develop the basic social skills necessary for emotional intimacy. These individuals tend to veer off into isolative lives and generally experience relief rather than loneliness from their avoidance of contact. And yet a third group may find themselves unhappily lonesome due to basic life circumstances over which they have little control, such as their physical distance from other people (e.g., remote rural living), being saddled with stay-at-home domestic obligations that leave little time for restorative socialization (e.g., being a single parent, or a grown child caring for an aging parent), or transportation limitations that make it impossible to get to where other people are (e.g., no car or public transportation available).

These different sources of interpersonal loneliness must be distinguished from what is known, in psychologist's circles, as "intrapersonal isolation," which is basically a psychological defense mechanism whereby an individual feels disconnected from their own authentic self due to compartmentalizing and repressing various "unacceptable" aspects of their inner world. This is not the emphasis here and not what we will be talking about when we use the word "isolation." Some degree of self-understanding and self-acceptance, that is, knowing and honoring one's authentic needs, feelings, and wishes, is presumed for overcoming social isolation. Without this, there is a risk of yielding to dysfunctional conformity by submerging the authentic self in exchange for a pretense of connection. This, as we shall see, is very different from the *true experience of connectedness and belonging.*

A further distinction must be made between interpersonal loneliness as a result of social isolation, and what we will refer to here as a more fundamental, inescapable, existential aloneness. While the individual subjective experience may be somewhat similar in both cases, and while interpersonal relating can sometimes help reduce the anxiety arising from our existential aloneness, it is useful to consider them separately. They stem from different sources and must ultimately be addressed from different stances. For no matter how closely and satisfyingly involved we are with others, there persists an underlying distance that can never be bridged. We are, in relation to others after all, different people with different lives to live. That we are each a separate individual point of view in the universe is an inescapable "given" of existence. If we are *not* a separate individual, with our own point of view, wishes, and motivations, then we are still, to that degree, merged with and subjugated to, some other external person or group or ideology in a less individuated way.

The notions of "attachment" and "separation/individuation" are useful to consider. We all want to feel connected and safe. We all want to feel that we belong to a group, a family, a community. At the same time, we want to be self-determining in life, and want to be encouraged and allowed to rely on our own judgment, and trusted to make our own decisions about how to best navigate our individual life toward happiness and success (however *we* define it). There is an inherent conflict here that all of us must struggle with—some people more than others, and during some stages of life (e.g., adolescence) more than others. But it is an ongoing task of living for us to find an acceptable balance between our separateness (as an individual) and our connectedness (as a member of collective life)—we need others, and we need solitude. Both are true and valid.

Unfortunately, the society we have currently co-created emphasizes an insidious combination of the worst of both. Our current socio-economic system encourages and rewards the least-desirable aspects of both ends of the spectrum, simultaneously. Our current social structures promote a dysfunctional form of individualism—an immature emphasis on self-centeredness, greed, and indifference toward the suffering of others—at one end of the spectrum. At the same time, these same structures promote a naïve, numbed out, compliant sort of conformity—the subjugation of "non-conformist" inclinations and the acceptance of choosing from a controlled palette of consumer options to "express one's individuality"—at the other end. These caricatures of individual and collective power are portrayed as desirable characteristics to which one should aspire. Yet these distorted depictions are both destructive of the individual as well as detrimental to the forward progress of society.

We've co-created a society in which people come and go in our lives with such frequency and aloofness that it sometimes feels like we're all perpetually "just passing through." At some level, I guess you could say we *are*. Yet for many, old established neighborhoods resonate with our longing for an era when families stayed put for multiple generations. Some of this still exists. But for the majority of twenty-first century Americans, life is much more transient. A study by the National Realtors Association reported that the average American moves every seven years. That's quite a churn rate. And the rate of change in our social institutions (e.g., school systems, government agencies, health care system, etc.) is staggering and overwhelming, even and especially for the people working within them, let alone the rest of us who depend on and are affected by them. In such a rapidly and constantly changing set of circumstances, hanging on to one's individuality becomes a matter of survival, lest you "fall through the cracks" of society and get "lost in the shuffle." But this form of individualism, in which we are encouraged to "be your own best friend" and "watch out for your own interests because nobody else will," extracts a huge cost from humanity. It exacerbates the inescapable existential loneliness with which we already struggle by reinforcing interpersonal isolation. This fragmentation of society—the decline of large extended families in stable residential neighborhoods, the shift away from shopping at locally owned and operated businesses, the disappearance of house-calling doctors, and the lack of opportunities for involvement in meaningful communal activities that are within walking distance of our homes—only increases our estrangement from each other. Beyond the loss of cultural enrichment and personal fulfillment, this loss may also diminish our prospects for collective survival in the years that lie ahead.

It's encouraging to know that we don't have to "go it alone" in life. And yet, at another level, we *do*. How can this be? A useful approach to this paradoxical dilemma can found in the development of a rational, mature mode of relating that honors both the individual and the collective as important aspects of an integrated, well-functioning life. Some ways of relating are more effective at providing a sense of connection and belonging than others. Human development, in the areas of emotional and moral maturity, can take us beyond merely trying to use others as a means to escape existential aloneness. And this is important because, as we have seen, it is not really possible to escape. We must come to grips with our separateness and individuate our personal stance and point of view, and learn to be comfortable with who *we* are in the universe so that we can then engage and enjoy others deeply and intimately without losing ourselves. It is possible to achieve and experience deep, meaningful social and emotional intimacy in healthy ways that don't require the submerging of our identity, beliefs, values, and so forth, in order to feel connected. Having faced and accepted that we must steer our own course in life, and having dealt reasonably well with the frightening aloneness that is implied, we find ourselves freed and empowered to join with others in genuine closeness without loss of boundaries. Mature relating requires that we are first able to be alone. But, finding and establishing our individual self in the universe doesn't mean that we have to sit at home by ourselves waiting for life to happen or for others to discover us.

The process of maturation moves us inexorably toward the recognition that we are, indeed, ultimately separate, self-determining individuals. We must learn to rely on our own resources and stand on our own feet with our chests high, and greet the world face to face. We may still sometimes feel anxious—we're human. We may still feel small or discouraged at times, and benefit from a hug. Fortunately, we are free to choose our own course, and we can choose to "do life" with great camaraderie, deep satisfying intimacy, and a tremendous sense of belonging if we wish. We can work at surrounding ourselves with supportive authentic relationships and conviviality that empower us to take a bold stance and reach for greatness. Upon acceptance of, and responsibility for, our ultimate aloneness, we are better able to turn toward others and relate with depth and honesty, and with an empathetic understanding that they, too, are alone and seeking connection in the pursuit of worthy aims. From one perspective, we are *all* homeless in the vast universe. From another, we are all connected. Thus the paradox. A little compassion for ourselves, and others, is in order.

Too much of life is wasted trying to deny existential isolation, rather than building the bridges that cross the chasms. Reciprocal caring goes a long way toward lessening the angst, and is a reliable source of encouragement for social change. Learning to hear each other's struggles and support each other in shedding old, conditioned, self-limiting patterns of behavior and internalized stereotypes is a viable path toward transcendence. Turning one's whole being toward another, with a conscious intention to understand and appreciate the uniqueness of *that* individual doesn't eliminate our separateness, but it does help to reduce the sense of isolation, even as it seems to benefit both parties. Caring, without expecting anything in return, is its own reward. Enjoyment can be found in witnessing the flourishing of another life. It's like watching a blossom unfold.

This is very different from trying to escape loneliness through dependence upon various distractions and diversions. The escapist strategy is ultimately futile, as we've seen. We cannot sufficiently lose ourselves in the pursuit and maintenance of material objects. We cannot sustain busy lives with hectic routines without collapsing into the void. Nor can we remain engaged in a continuous stream of entertainment without eventually losing interest in the shallowness of the relief. Every time we let up the pace, every time we come up for air, we find that the vast empty universe—and our aloneness in it—is still there. Every time we get high, we come down. Every time we "find it," we lose it. Every time we conform to some group's expectations and find some temporary relief and a sense of belonging, we eventually bump into the incongruities between that group's aims/beliefs/customs, and our authentic self. As the unacceptable differences become undeniably highlighted, we must either move on or stay connected in a less-fully present way through a false appearance of conformity. And woe be unto those who seek union through compulsive sexual behavior, as the emptiness is only amplified in the aftermath. Interpersonal union need not be sought in an escapist or addictive manner.

So then, how does this all relate to talking across the divides in our everyday lives about the challenges we face as a civilization? Well, we need to take into account that the good humans we are talking with are, at some level, like all of us, feeling very alone in the universe. We don't want to stoke that particular feeling to the detriment of the conversation. We don't want to trigger characteristic defense mechanisms, and we don't want to reinforce a rigidly held worldview that might be contrary to taking in new information or re-thinking how one might better proceed at this critical juncture.

It's important to note, that while different people react to existential anxiety, in this case stemming from inescapable aloneness, in different ways, it is the *relationship*—your relationship with them, one-to-one, at the very moment of your conversation—that is the *key* to helping them consider a different vision. Your ability to help them feel safe and connected and appreciated during your dialogue is *the* factor which will decrease their interpersonal loneliness (and related anxiety) enough that it will be possible for them to let go and "drift" (imaginatively) into new areas of thought—exploring new possibilities for a different type of future together. Out of this connection comes an understanding that making sure each other's children get fed in the future is preferable to killing each other over scarce supplies. Relaxation occurs between you. Your backs feel covered by each other. Suspicion dissolves, tension deflates, tightening loosens, and gentle smiles and sighs are exchanged—"We are on the same side, after all." The isolation has been temporarily assuaged.

As this effort to extend good will continues and spreads among those who have been lovingly enough encountered, and whose best thinking has been intelligently incorporated into the collective wisdom, an organically growing community emerges, one by one, which simultaneously provides that desired sense of belonging, while also increasing the survival-oriented behavior of the group. Society moves forward by coordinating efforts and intelligence in a constructive manner. A new culture emerges that is more sustainable and more effective at fulfilling rational human needs. A sense of unity with diversity gives strength, resourcefulness, and resilience to a global civilization and a new "people over profit" era.

Part One

Why The Book?

The current cultural momentum is:

- unsustainable
- unsatisfying
- conditioned
- fear and greed based
- changeable, but...

- Personal Growth
- Moral Maturity
- Social Evolution
- Human Potential

Part Two

Three Things

Understand the person you are talking with:

- **Section One**
  their unique
  CHARACTER STYLE

- **Section Two**
  their
  CURRENT WORLDVIEW

- **Section Three**
  which
  EXISTENTIAL CONCERN
  they are struggling with

Part Three

Techniques

You might try:

- listening
- "between the lines"
- parallel their arguments
- question assumptions
- change the context
- stick to common ground
- applaud all steps
- other ideas...

Part Four

Examples

Imagine yourself in:

- An Awkward Event
- A Workplace Conflict
- Air Travel Delay

PART THREE

What To Do

Introduction

HOPEFULLY, BY THIS POINT I'VE BEEN ABLE TO CONVEY WHY I THINK A BOOK about communicating across the divides in our everyday lives is important. And, hopefully, I've been able to illuminate some of the difficulties that arise in undertaking this endeavor. We face multiple challenges, as a civilization, at this historical juncture. And we need to find ways to join our best collective thinking in the noble pursuit of conscious social evolution toward a truly sustainable and more satisfying future together on this one planet that we all share.

To that end, Part Three will begin with a summary of those dynamics from Part Two that we've seen to be potentially problematic to moving forward in a coordinated, cooperative manner. Next, we'll look at what I consider to be some of the *general* considerations to be taken into account when devising a communication strategy for dealing with a particularly difficult conversation. Then, we'll consider a number of *specific techniques* that might be of use in one situation or another.

Part Four of the book will present a few hypothetical examples of how these techniques *might* be applied.

A Brief Summary of Part Two

I WANT TO BEGIN THIS SUMMARY BY SAYING, ONCE MORE, THAT IT HAS BEEN
with some trepidation that I undertook the writing of this book. I have a
concern that the characterizations presented in Part Two might be misused
to label and divide people against each other, rather than used to increase
understanding, empathy, and connection around shared values, concerns,
experiences, and aspirations.

It is my sincere hope that those who read this material will remain alert to
their own potential to forget that individual people are not simply a collection
of conditioned patterns of thinking, feeling, and behaving. Each person's
essential nature is much *more* than that. Each individual's potential is much
larger and more flexible than their conditioned, characteristic ways of moving
through life. The consciousness I speak of, which is our most essential *being*-
ness, is able to hold, appreciate, and grow through multiple worldviews
in a lifetime. Our essential nature is big enough to face and embrace the
uncertainty of life, and to manage the discomfort of the "givens" of existence,
without resorting to destructive, unaware behavior. The essential self that
we fundamentally *are*, is unfolding and evolving continuously. Life is moving
forward *through* us, toward ever-greater, integrated complexity and cooperation, and we are a part of it.

So then, with that disclaimer in place, here is a short review of what we
examined in Part Two. We saw that we are all anxious, at any given moment,
whether we are conscious of it or not. Anxiety is a part of existence. Life is
uncertain. And when we talk about (remind each other of) the uncertainties
of life, it often increases the intensity of that anxiety. This doesn't feel good.
Our tendency is to seek relief by resorting to various individual (characterological) modes of managing personal discomfort, some of which can result
in highly unsustainable, unkind, and unintelligent behavior. We've also seen
how these mechanisms that we have developed to ward off individual anxiety
occur within the context of our current worldview. And we've seen that all
worldviews provide some sense of coherence in an otherwise chaotic existence

that lacks meaning and consistency. We looked at how presenting information that challenges a person's worldview "rocks" their grasp on reality, and can be experienced as very threatening. Without something to hold on to that helps give life meaning, we run smack up against the big void and all that is implied by the realization that life can be short and harsh, that we are left on our own to grind out a few grueling decades in a cold, empty, meaningless, uncaring universe, and then we die. Ouch! But, also, as we've seen, there is more than just this. While the facts of existence are, without a doubt, bleak and hopeless from the perspective of our limited, individual ego, we can also see that it is primarily *from* this limited vantage point that our suffering arises. When our identity rests in a larger "spiritual" perspective within which all of this is unfolding, we often find that our ego is freed and can more easily shed its old conditioning and worldviews. The individual ego can then serve as a healthy, useful tool for continued personal and social transformation.

So, to sum up Part Two in a nutshell, any (character) type of person can be found to be operating within any worldview, and can be experiencing any type of existential anxiety at any given moment. Our habitual (individual and collective) ways of attempting to manage this anxiety most often add to our confusion, suffering, and unsustainable behaviors. These self-defeating momentums can, and must, be outgrown developmentally as a civilization, so that we might move forward together toward a better future.

Devising a Communication Strategy

General Considerations

IF THE GOAL OF THIS BOOK IS TO INCREASE THE EFFECTIVENESS OF YOUR communications across the divides in your everyday life, then the trick to doing so lies in consciously working at it. Yes, it takes some effort and careful attention to thoughtfully put the pieces together in your mind before a picture of who you're talking to comes into focus. As you think about that person, and listen closely, you'll find that your mind begins to assemble a coherent understanding of how they think (their characteristic mode), where they're coming from (their worldview), and what they're really feeling nervous about (their existential angst). This will help you understand what they will be capable of hearing, and what they will reject and defend against. It will give you a way of understanding how to best appreciate them for who they are. Please keep in mind that you are not their therapist and they are not paying you for a diagnosis, so keep that part to yourself. It won't be helpful. What *will* be helpful, is to think—in the moment if you can, or upon reflection later, for a subsequent dialogue—about how to best approach them in a way that leaves them feeling valued and supported for who they are, and for how they see the world, *even as you present a different view.*

You might begin by considering their *character type.* How closely do they fit one or more of the types presented earlier? What do we know about *not* getting on the wrong side of someone who moves through life in that way? Next, consider their *worldview.* Which general approach to life are they espousing (coming from)? And finally, which of the inescapable, but normally denied, anxieties seems to be currently aroused and prominent in their experience? Answers to these questions will inform you about how they are likely to hear your concerns and defend themselves. This should help illuminate strategies that you might try in order to avoid causing rigidification of their stance—what you need to be careful about in order to not offend them, how you might make your position more appealing, and how to offer a palliative perspective for holding the discomfort involved when considering these difficult topics.

I find it helpful to think in terms of testing tentative hypotheses about the person I am speaking with as the conversation proceeds. You try something out, then you listen for feedback to learn whether your comment has helpful or not. Have they relaxed a bit? Do they seem interested in considering what you are saying? Do you seem to be getting through or not? Does it appear that you are contributing to the expansion of knowledge or awareness? Or are they becoming tighter and more shrill in their (unspoken and spoken) reactions to what you've said? You have to keep your own reactions in check, so that you can remain open and connected, and listen to and think about them and the conversation as it is happening.

This is the work. It takes effort. If you want to increase your chances for a successful interchange, I recommend doing some thinking and strategizing ahead of time about particular individuals and particular topics you want to address. Get out a pencil and paper and do the work. Think about the person. Try to identify, specifically, their characteristic ways of interacting, that is, their character type, their worldview, and which existential anxieties you think will most likely be aroused by your conversation. Take your time and think it through. Question your own assumptions based on the fact that you find *their* "type" disagreeable to *your* "type." (There's plenty of growth here for all of us.) Take all the time you need. Then go the next step and develop a few hypotheses—"If I say *this*, and they respond with *that*, then it probably means such-and-so." You can then "test" those hypotheses in your conversation with them. You may also find that this will help you to stay more conscious, positive, and supportive because you won't be as likely to react to *their* comments or invalidations of *your* position.

A useful perspective, I find, is to keep in mind that *everyone* is capable of higher functioning. *Everyone.* (Yes, even your least favorite person.) Everyone is capable of growing and developing. We are *all* in a continuous, ongoing process of *becoming*—evolving toward greater awareness and maturity—even when we appear "stuck" at various stages. We can, if we choose, help each other *become* what is next for us (developmentally) so that we can take our place in the forward march of civilization toward an ever greater existence as a species.

Devising a Communication Strategy

Specific Techniques

FIRST, A PRECAUTIONARY WORD ABOUT TECHNIQUES.

Basically, any time we're relying on a technique, we're being somewhat less present in-the-moment for the person we're talking with. This is, perhaps, the most fundamental mistake in communication.

When we learn a technique and recall it and try to apply it in a *living* situation, it's too easy to miss what's happening between us and the other person *in that very moment*, because we're off in our head trying to remember how to do it, and how to make it fit this particular person and situation.

It's useful to *not* think of techniques as being one-size-fits-all. It's better to consider them as potentially helpful guidelines for adjusting one's approach on-the-fly, as ways to help you stay closely connected and supportively present with the other person.

While there are probably better ways, and less-effective ways to approach any situation, there is really no one correct technique that can be known before-hand, memorized, recalled, and applied mechanically to get you off-the-hook and out of a difficult exchange. It's tempting to think that we can rely on an arsenal of techniques to help us when our own feelings get hurt and our characteristic defensive maneuvers are reactivated by what the other person has just said. But what works far better is to strive to be as *present* and accepting of ourselves, and the other, as we can. Keep making the effort to return to that spacious, relaxed, appreciative awareness over and over again as the dialogue unfolds. Each and every moment, each and every unexpected twist and turn, each and every challenging, embarrassing, frightening moment is an opportunity to stay ever-fresh in our presence and thinking.

Techniques, in this light, can be seen as places to come *from* into dialogue, rather than *things* to wield against others. With that said, let's begin by looking at the most basic technique: listening well.

Listen: Talk Less—Listen More

You have the right to remain silent. Consider doing so.

In general, it's often helpful when engaged in dialogue across a divide to talk less and listen more. Talk less, listen more. That sounds like a pretty simple thing to do, but … try it. Try just listening. With full in-the-moment presence, without judgment, without trying to change or control what the other person is saying, without rehearsing a defensive response in your mind while they're talking. Just listen. With a welcoming smile and attitude, if possible. This can be a powerful gesture of your acceptance of them as a person. It also carries an implied invitation for them to consider whether fortifying and defending their position is really necessary.

Doing anything at all, externally or internally, other than simply listening attentively, can take you away from being present in-the-moment with awareness. This is not to negate that sometimes it can be helpful to think to yourself, internally, about how similar this person is to you: that they suffer as a human being, from all the same losses and uncertainties, just like you; that they want to feel accepted and valued as a person, just like you; that they become afraid and defensive when they feel their values and beliefs are being challenged, or that the structures upon which they have based their life are crumbling, just like you. This is the basis of compassionate listening. And, just like you, they need to be listened to with awareness and acceptance. Nobody wants to feel that how they have been living is "wrong." So … talk less, listen more. This is a safe prescription for not fouling up our fundamental human-to-human relatedness. It's a good fall-back position when you find yourself confused about where the dialogue is heading, or when you've gotten "off track" and the situation feels "tighter" and less harmonious. Go back to just listening, with a smile. And allow the connection to be reaffirmed. This is basic.

Listen (respectfully) "Between the Lines"

A fundamental premise of psychoanalytic inquiry is that the words that come out of our mouths are laden with more meaning than we are generally aware of—thus the notions of conscious and unconscious. If you take a moment and think of your date of birth, what you have just done is recall a piece of "mental content" (a thought in this case) from your unconscious to your conscious awareness. Repression (as well as suppression and most of the other psychological maneuvers that we examined earlier as our characterological ego-defense mechanisms) aims to keep mental contents out of awareness. Repression is simply the habitual blocking from consciousness of mental contents such as ideas, images, remembrances, and so forth. Repression is an admirable defense. It allows us (as an individual ego) to function in the daily world. It automatically puts to rest a disturbing dream shortly after awakening so that we can brush our teeth and get to work on time. If the repressive barrier is easily bypassed as a result of our desire to remember or understand, then that piece of mental content is said to exist in our "preconscious." Such was the case with your birth date. It is available for recall without too much effort. Contents that are heavily repressed may take years of analysis to recover, if ever they are allowed access to awareness. They are said to be "deeply" unconscious.

When we speak, what we say, how we say it, and why we say it at that particular moment all reveal underlying meaning. If we listen closely enough, we can begin to hear how people's words often contain "hidden" (unconscious) indications about how they size up the world, and how they navigate through life. If we listen attentively enough, and if we are able to make the situation feel "safe" enough, by appreciating rather than attacking them, and seeing that their thoughts, opinions, and beliefs are not *them*, that is, not who they *are*, but are merely mental contents that they *have*, then, a very interesting thing can begin to occur. In subtle and sometimes symbolic ways, people will begin to communicate their underlying feelings, needs, wishes, and so forth. Seemingly fragmented bits and images will come together, like a puzzle, and coalesce into patterns in your *own* (preconscious) mind to form a coherent picture of the person you are speaking with. You will begin to hear (and see) more and more clearly, beneath what they are saying, how *what* they are saying reveals their individual character type, the worldview within which they currently find themselves operating, and which existential anxiety they are wrestling with *in this moment*. If you follow this thread, it generally becomes increasingly evident that everything they say is being shaped by and derived from these underlying conditioned sentiments. This gives you workable hypotheses to test out by making simple statements of validation and support for who they are, and how they struggle in life, as you attempt to move the dialogue forward.

This requires dividing your conscious attention between multiple levels, and staying very present in the here-and-now with yourself, as well as with the other person—while also formulating hypotheses about what's occurring between you. It means listening to, and thinking about, the person with whom you are speaking at the same time that you are monitoring your own physiological, emotional, and psychological processes. As the seemingly fragmented material they are presenting begins to coalesce around themes in your mind and crystallize into recognizable forms and shapes, your hypotheses about what's going on can be formulated into little "tests" which are either confirmed or disconfirmed by further listening, that is, by noting their reactions to what *you* say. As you listen closely, think about the dialogue you are having, and test your hypotheses; you will gain understanding about how their defensiveness follows a fairly predictable pattern (character type), and that their opinions speak to a coherent set of values (worldview). Keep listening and you'll hear which underlying existential concern(s) they are struggling with in.

When you think you have a clear enough picture of how their ego operates in the world (their character type), how they see the world (including you), and what their deepest concern is at this moment (existential fear), then you can then try tailoring your communicative response to what they are saying, so that it speaks to these underlying dynamics in a way that communicates acceptance, reassurance, understanding, and appreciation for them as an individual (if not for their opinion) at the same time that it gently nudges their thinking forward.

This is a skill. Like all skills, it gets better the more you practice it. Skills become habits when practiced enough. They become unconscious ways of behaving so that you don't have to consciously try so hard after while. Some people are more gifted than others at doing this, but everyone has the capability of improving the accuracy of their compassion and their dialogue skills. This, in my opinion, is a valuable communication technique to develop for those individuals who are interested in community building and social change.

Parallel Their Arguments Without Agreeing

This technique is a little more consciously manipulative than appreciative "deep" listening. With this technique, you are allowing the person to present their argument, make it clear that you are listening and understand what they are saying, but not necessarily agreeing or disagreeing with them. Just let them talk until they run out of steam. Simply let them have their say and then repeat back to them what they have said in your own words, so that they feel heard. The word "parallel" is being used here as a verb—it is something that you *do*. You *parallel* their argument without resisting it—without giving it anything to push against. It's the verbal version of the martial arts notion of moving in the same direction as the attack that is coming at you. You use *their* force to your ends. You side-step the assault and allow them to fall forward under their own momentum.[1]

For example, let's say you're speaking with someone you care about and they're talking on and on about how a certain AM radio talk show host, who you think spurs division among people, would make a great presidential candidate. You might simply respond by saying something like, "Oh. So you think so-and-so would make a good presidential candidate. I'm interested to hear why you think so."

Like milking venom from a snake's fangs, you invite them to drain off all the toxic justifications and aggressive posturing that accompanies and defends their vulnerability—listening, always (as indicated earlier) for the underlying unconscious feelings and meaning revealed by their words.

You simply stay connected and present (in the moment) with them, while maintaining a *parallel* stance in relation to their argument, rather than op-posing them or invalidating their argument. You assume a stance that looks in the same direction as their argument is pointing until they exhaust their defensiveness and become aware, on their own, of how exaggeratedly absurd and unsupportable, or petty, or mean-spirited they must sound. Given enough room to air their position, the contradictions within their venting will tend to become increasingly obvious. Any self-centered, callous indifference toward others will stand out as undeniable. *Don't*, however, point it out to them. That will just instigate the need to continue defending their stance. Let them, instead, just run out of steam and drive themselves into a dead-end. Just stay with them—"Oh, uh huh, is that so?" You're not agreeing, and you're not silently condoning their conclusions. You're just acknowledging that they have a point of view, and you're giving them room to explore it out loud and hear how it sounds.

When they arrive at the "logical conclusion" of a particular line of reasoning such as, "Well, of *course* I'm gonna vote in favor of my own economic self interest. Who wouldn't? I mean, who cares about welfare recipients? They're scum. They should stop taking drugs and get a job." At this juncture, the parallel strategy would be to lean in and nod while saying something like, "Sometimes it seems like people should try harder and not expect others to pay their way." Or, "Sometimes it's frustrating to be working so hard at trying to get ahead when others seem to be getting a free ride." Or, "Voting for one's own interests can sometimes seem like the right thing to do, especially when it seems like others are getting away with not doing their share." Something like that.

Then, back to more listening. Just keep listening. Your parallel response will likely set off another round of venting. Let them continue to vent and drain off their negativity and defensiveness. Just keep validating how it feels to them *without* agreeing with their position. It's not *your* position, but they have a right to have it be *their* position. This is the implied message. The hardest part of doing this is not reacting to what they are saying—not having your *own* reactions take over your ability to stay present and connected in the moment. You need to make it feel safe enough for them to get it all out, every last drop, without saying anything that might be perceived as subtly critical or defensive. You don't want to trigger them to further fortification.

Hear them out. Listen to their blaming and bigoted scapegoating, their paranoid accusations and pop-culture corporate-sponsored media sound bites without taking it as an attack of *you*. Stay parallel to their thrust. Side step the intensity and let it go past you.

The hope is, if you can give them enough time and supportive attention to express their frustrations and fears, that maybe at some point, if not now then perhaps later in a more relaxed private moment, they may begin to hear for themselves how racist, sexist, classist, and so forth, their stance really *is*. They may begin to recognize how entitled and indifferent they really sound, and how that keeps them feeling bitter and separated from the connected-ness with others that they really long for, and how this results in a pretty darn unsatisfying life.

Most people, the good humans that we all are underneath, will eventually notice, all by ourselves, how arrogant and unkind we sound. Like that martial arts technique of moving *with* the energy instead of against it, if you don't provide anything solid for them to resist or push against, their offensive thrust will eventually collapse and fall flat, leaving them—aggression exhausted —up against the empty silence and your welcoming smile. In that receptive, non-opposing emptiness, they will have the opportunity to hear the reverber-ations of their own strident opinions. They will be able to hear them, because there is no other "noise" to compete with, or to frighten them. They can feel their connection with you in that moment. You are there for *them* as a fundamentally good human being who mostly wants the same things they do. They sense that you see and accept *them* (their essential self) as someone quite different than, larger than, more beneficent than their sometimes confused ways of moving through life and trying to make sense of it. They feel their connectedness with you and, since separation is an illusion, this is a big step in the right direction. Feeling valued for who they *are* at their most essential level, and receiving acknowledgement for how things "add up" for them at the moment, makes conversing with you a safe place from which to explore other possibilities in life.

---

[1] Note that this technique is different from the more common "reverse psychology" or "paradoxical intention" techniques sometimes used in clinical practice.

Question Their Underlying Assumptions
—as Non-judgmentally as You Can

We all make assumptions. We base our lives on assumptions. For example, we assume we will be alive tomorrow. We are aware of some of our assumptions; others are quite unconscious. We obviously favor those assumptions that, in our estimation, offer us the best chances of survival and satisfaction in life. Our assumptions might be based on probability (scientific facts); beliefs (religion/worldview); our unique personal history (experiences in our life to date), or other sources—"Somebody told me one time that...." (see sidebar on page 178)

Most middle-class Americans, for example, assume that they will wake up tomorrow into relatively peaceful circumstances. We assume, for example, that 9-11, anthrax, and random acts of violence are not everyday occurrences, that we will have enough (probably too much) food to eat, and that we will enjoy the privileges and rights of citizenship (life, liberty, and the pursuit of happiness). All of these are assumptions.

The aim of this technique is to respectfully raise questions in the other person's mind about their underlying assumptions, so that they can reconsider the assumptions upon which their beliefs and behavior are built. You might say something like, "So, it sounds like you believe that global climate change is a hoax." Or, "It seems like you think peak oil will never really be much of an issue for you personally."

When someone questions our assumptions, it rattles us. It disrupts the stability of what might be called our "assumptive state." It calls into question the basis of our assumptions, and, more importantly, raises to awareness the fact that we are *all* operating from a set of assumptions.

This is important to keep in mind when questioning people's assumptions. It's important to proceed gently and respectfully, without criticism or invalidation of their assumptions. What you're trying to do is help them to become aware that they are making assumptions, so that they can see them and evaluate them against other views of reality—"Do *these* assumptions really reflect my best thinking and heartfelt values? Do they motivate me to proceed in the direction I *really* want to go in life?"

As with change at the level of core beliefs, change at the level of assumptions can be very profound. Reexamination of one's core beliefs and underlying assumptions can result in whole sections of one's life dropping away as no longer relevant or significant as new horizons appear and become more appealing. This is the process of personal (emotional, psychological, spiritual) growth: recognizing and honoring how what *was* important has served its purpose to bring you to this point, where letting go of the old and embracing the new moves you yet another step forward, developmentally.

Different assumptions lead to different outcomes. A person whose assumption is that infinite population growth with continually higher material living standards on a finite planet *is* possible, is likely to make very different behavioral choices than someone who assumes that per capita consumption of material resources exists within the biological limits of the planet. Assuming that there is an endless supply of oil; that technology will "pull the rabbit out of the hat" and come up with some new inexpensive energy source that will allow for continued rampant growth and expansion of the economy without a period of hardship during the transition; that there are plenty of fish in the sea; that the earth can support ten times as many people at a much higher standard of living; that more *is* better. These sorts of assumptions will result in very different outcomes for our global civilization than assumptions that acknowledge the externalized costs to underprivileged peoples in far-away lands, and the ecological destruction required to support such assumptions.

Here are a few of the more common underlying assumptions that I have run into in my attempts to dialogue across the divide about the challenges we face as a global community. I hope you will take these as starting points for listening and add to this list those you discover as you venture forth.

… that there are enough natural resources for China, India, and other emerging nations to live an American-style "middle-class" consumer-oriented lifestyle

… that war is inevitable

… that competition between people and nations is good and inevitable (rather than working toward intelligently coordinated cooperation that maximizes quality of life for more people)

... that global (so-called) "free market" capitalism in its current form is the best possible economic system for humanity going forward

... that "our way of life" is what everyone should want and strive for

... that material wealth is correlated with happiness in a never-ending, upward ascent

... that people get what they deserve (i.e., poor people deserve to be poor) and that privilege doesn't exist in our "free" society

... that the corporate-sponsored pop-culture media give an accurate representation of reality (rather than simply one version of the truth—a version that serves profit-maximization for owning-class interests and perpetuates many forms of social oppression)

... that pollution, resource depletion, peak oil, global climate change, and so forth, are just hoaxes (not really happening) invented by discontented people who want to wreck the economy

... that biological/ecological limits to growth do not exist, or at least will not affect me or "my people" and certainly not in our lifetimes

... that sharing and cooperating is equivalent to "heavy-handed, Soviet-style communism that has already proven itself to be a disaster"

... that individualism (rather than concern for the collective good) is inevitable and the best approach to life

... that the status quo is good and that change is bad and threatening, rather than that change is an opportunity to make life better for ourselves and future generations.

ASSUMPTIONS VERSUS TRUTH

Both science and religion are based on assumptions. Each can be used to argue either side of any argument. This is why, generally, they are not very helpful foundations for dialogue when attempting to talk across a divide. The assumptions of both science and religion limit their usefulness and appeal, especially to proponents of the *other* ideology. Better, I think, to respectfully raise to awareness whatever assumptions are being relied on, than to challenge them. Also, I think it's hard to know, in the moment, whether your dialogue is having much of an effect or not. Sometimes, just having one's assumptions brought to awareness in an accepting, receptive relationship is enough to permit a change of view to occur—upon later reflection, in the privacy of one's own thinking.

Change the Context of the Dialogue

Psychoanalytic interpretation is a time-honored therapeutic intervention. In the therapy setting, interpretation is more accurately understood as *reinterpretation*. The client expresses feelings, concerns, and conclusions about their circumstances. The therapist offers a reinterpretation of the client's circumstances and experience. Because the therapist's view differs from the client's view, the client is now posed with the challenge of reconciling their old view with the therapist's different way of looking at things. The therapist's reinterpretation "reframes" the client's situation, offering an opportunity to reconsider previous conclusions. The same situation is now seen in a new light. Circumstances are held in a new context from which a different meaning might be derived. It is hoped that the reinterpreted view offered by the therapist will be helpful to the client. In psychotherapeutic practice, tentative and concise reinterpretations are generally best. When talking across the divides in our daily lives, a slightly more insistent variation of this same technique can sometimes be applied. Hopefully, here too, the result will be beneficial.[1]

It's important to keep in mind that when another person's reinterpretation of our assessment of reality is accurate, it can "sting" and stir up discomfort and resistance. It's psychologically disruptive when our previously held interpretation of "how things *are*" has been laid bare by an obviously more accurate way of looking at the situation. For example, it can sometimes be embarrassing when it is made apparent that our underlying motivations might *not* have been as benevolent as we had hoped to convince others. This "revealing" generally leads to some measure of defensiveness in the characteristic ways we have explored in previous chapters.

For the purposes of this book, the basic approach to reinterpreting reality goes something like this. Let's say the person with whom you are talking goes on and on about how war is good for the economy, war is inevitable, war is justified in this instance, and so forth. Your relaxed, polite response might simply offer a different interpretation. You subtly shift the *context* of the conversation by talking, instead, about the value of diplomacy throughout history, the benefits to humanity of cooperative efforts, and the great cultural achievements of peace-time economic growth. You don't use the word war.

You don't converse within that context. Instead, you focus on words like *peace* and *cooperation* and *diplomacy*. You're not talking about ending war, or why war is bad. You're talking about the benefits of peace and how peace is what everybody ultimately wants. *Peace* is the word you keep turning to. It's not that war is bad (although it is), it's that peace is *good*. If you keep using *their* words, the dialogue will reinforce a certain way of seeing things—a way that leads to predictable conclusions about what is possible and inevitable. By subtly shifting the context, by defining the situation with *different* words, you open up new possibilities for agreement.

The same general approach can be applied to all of the issues that divide us. For example, there is a real difference between talking about how unfortunate, but inevitable, toxic pollution is for economic growth, and talking about the desirability of clean water. These different contexts for dialogue lead to very different thinking and conclusions about what is possible.

It's worth taking some time to sit down, think through, and even write out the various justifications you run into with particular people. Think of ways to change the context of those discussions so that they align with *your* values and vision. Try to find the words that roll off your tongue easily. Learning to clearly articulate what you are *for* with words that evoke the desired context, is a part of changing the dialogue (and consciousness) that needs to occur in society at large. (see FOR words on page 35)

Basically you're trying to find ways of communicating your concerns that make it possible for the other person to step outside their usual way of viewing reality—their usual context or interpretation of the "facts." By subtly changing the words, you make it possible for them to see things from a different angle—*your* angle, *your* way of interpreting reality. I mean, come on, who's not for clean water? Once you're both seeing things from the same angle—one in which new possibilities exist—then combining your thinking to explore collaborative solutions is *much* easier.

"But," you might say, "isn't this manipulative?" Well, yes, it certainly is—to some degree. It's what might be called "framing the debate" in divisive win-lose political terminology. But the difference, here, is that you're not trying to *win* by defeating the other person or making them wrong. You're simply trying to elicit your *best combined thinking* toward a win-win solution. You're inviting them to explore a concern that, perhaps, might be more easily understood using a particular terminology. You're politely inviting them to take another look at the situation from a slightly different angle.

Thinking of it as a dialogue rather than a debate, and thoughtfully setting the context by being very conscious of the words you choose to describe the issue under discussion, is an intelligent attempt to encourage cooperation. It's an attempt to keep the discussion aimed in a productive direction by avoiding certain known impasses. It's an attempt to elicit and illuminate new thinking and fresh possibilities for moving forward together. The aim is to promote a context of *unity with diversity* that enables progress toward a better future together. This is very different than "beating" the other side.

By consciously attending to the context of the discussion, you avoid getting stuck arguing over narrow, rigidly held beliefs and tightening your stances around points of disagreement. By refocusing on words that indicate what you are *for* rather than against, you invite fresh thinking and collaboration around positive possibilities. It's important to steer away from words that evoke disdainful media-induced stereotypes. You can reduce resistance to exploring new solutions by avoiding words that might suggest "sacrifice" or "loss." For example, people are much less agreeable to talking about having to drive less than about the health benefits of walking and enjoying local community more. In general, people don't consider progress to include anything that limits their freedoms (e.g., more regulation), or that costs them more money (e.g., higher taxes). Anything that questions the legitimacy of authority to protect their property, or that raises issues of oppression or inequality in areas where they are privileged (such as socio-economic class, race, gender, etc.) will likely be met with resistance. If you understand their way of thinking—their way of holding the "facts" and deriving conclusions about what possibilities are realistic to pursue—then you will have some basis for predicting their reactions to your reinterpretation of reality. Your aim is to keep your thinking ahead of theirs so that you're not triggering their resistance, and you're not constantly trying to argue your way out of *their* context. Rather, you gently invite them to consider a different context that offers additional possibilities that they might not have considered before— possibilities that you might both find agreeable, a vision that appeals because it is framed correctly, and that leads to further imagining of hopeful possibilities.

From this collaborative vision, obvious next steps may reveal themselves. This is the path of progress.

---

[1] George Lakoff and the Rockridge Institute have done a lot of good work on reframing progressive issues for political debate. I encourage the reader to explore their excellent offerings. Some of what I have written here is more fully elaborated there, with less of my personal, psychoanalytic, and environmental biases.

Stick Together: Stick to Values You Both Share

The previous technique focused on changing the context of a discussion from debate to dialogue, from a win-lose argument to a cooperative exploration, from the inevitability of negative outcomes to the possibility of a brighter future. This feeling of being on the same side and working *together* for a better future can be enhanced and extended by consciously identifying your common ground. Cultivating a collaborative feeling between you is strengthened by affirming *together* where your circles of interest overlap—naming out loud those shared values and underlying wishes that represent your deepest, common human longings. What are those aspects of life that you *both* hold dear? What is it that you both agree is *really* important?

While these two techniques—changing the context of the dialogue, and sticking to mutual values—share the common goal of reaching some level of agreement between you, it is, perhaps, useful to consider them separately, as different approaches for increasing the effectiveness of our conversations across the divides in our lives.

The technique discussed here is based on an assumption that what we have in common, as human beings, is much more fundamental and important than what we allow to divide us. While there might be an infinite number of lesser differences that we, unfortunately, too frequently argue over, there are a number of more substantial, central core issues that we all share as human beings. Those sentiments that unite us tend to be greater in number than we recognize, while those issues that divide us are frequently less significant than we fear.

What is it that we all want? Our basic human longings include things like: a desire to love and feel loved; wanting to feel like we *belong* somewhere— to some social group, family, community—as a balance to our sense of isolation and our need for privacy; a need to feel safe and secure; a desire to see our children and grandchildren thrive and enjoy an easier life than the one we had; to feel that what we do in life is of some value or importance; access to uncontaminated food, water, and basic creature comforts (not too cold, not too hot, a comfortable place to sleep, etc.); the freedom to make choices and have some measure of control over our circumstances; and the ability to indulge our natural curiosity and feel as if we're continually learning new things, growing, developing new capabilities, or gaining and advancing in life rather than feeling stuck and limited by our circumstances. We want to feel that if we work hard and play by the rules that we can make our life better. We seem to share a common desire for fair, efficient, understandable governance (transparent and not overly complex); access to the best possible health care; and a prosperous economy that enables everyone to have the material security and comfort to enjoy a reasonably happy life. Beyond that, who wouldn't want abundant, affordable, clean, renewable energy? These desires are not so outrageous as to be denied or considered unattainable. We have ample intelligence, as a species, to pursue such interests fruitfully.

So where, then, do we get off track? How is it that we lose our way from knowing what it is that we all seem to desire, to actually *having* it as the reality of our collective lives? Where do we run into trouble? Well, the devil is in the details. "The Tragedy of the Commons" and other such conflicts between individual interest and collective benefit come into play. Translating shared common longings into mutually acceptable policies requires patience, compromise, and compassion—three qualities that are neither commonly promoted as desirable nor consistently reinforced by "the American way of life." We can change this. We can decide that we want to organize ourselves differently as a society, as a global community. We *are* the co-creators of the systems in which we live. We *can* have it the way we want it, by choosing and acting differently. We can co-create a global civilization that truly meets the rational, central needs of humanity, rather than serving the more abstract, less-satisfying goals of profit for the few at the expense of social and environmental exploitation.

How do we move in that direction?

The basic "technique" here is to just keep coming back to the common ground. Each time you find yourself snagged in a quarrel about differences, simply return to areas where your individual circles overlap. Continue to reconvene around shared values, common interests, and basic human longings. Rest in that connection; bask in that safe, good feeling of commonality between you. Take some deep breaths together, with a "pleased to be with you" feeling and look on your face. Then, ever so slowly venture outward again, "holding hands" (metaphorically or literally) as you vision your way forward, toward possibilities, toward solutions, in a way that honors and maintains that special, deeper human connection between you. Don't go any faster or any farther than you can stay connected and delighted to be with each other. Relationships are the foundational fabric of our lives, the essential cornerstones of our families, communities, and workplaces. Relationships are the source of power in our lives for social change and for fulfillment.

United we stand. We must affirm our connectedness across the divides in our lives. United we enjoy a much better chance of reaching our collective vision and meeting our basic human needs. We all want to be part of a safe, healthy, enjoyable, fair, prosperous society with upward potential. You can be confident and relaxed in knowing that. The practical details of how we get there can be worked out when approached with good will, sincere intentions, trust, honesty, and a cooperative spirit from "all sides." The current socio-economic-political system has been created by humans. What comes next in the continuous evolution of civilization will also be the result of our combined choices and actions. Human intelligence is innovative by nature. It is within our grasp to cooperate for our own good and to co-create a better next chapter in our collective saga.

Encourage and Applaud Steps in the Right Direction

If you want to train your dog to jump through a hoop, one method is to hold a hoop out to the side and say, "Jump through the hoop." When the dog looks at the hoop instead of you, you say, "Good dog!" You reach into your pocket with the other hand and pull out a doggie treat as a reward. Then you do it again. You do this over and over until the dog clearly understands that when you say, "Jump through the hoop," the reward follows looking at the hoop. Then, gradually, you change the game by waiting to reward the dog until it pokes the hoop with its nose. The dog is communicating to you—"See, I know it's *this* thing in your hand that brings me the reward." "Good dog!" You reward the dog for not just looking at the hoop, but going a little further and actually poking the hoop with its nose. Repeat this over and over until the nose-poking behavior is firmly established. Then, once again, you slightly shift the target behavior a little further toward jumping through the hoop. This time the reward comes only after the dog has poked the hoop with its nose *and* raises a paw in the direction of the hoop—"Good dog!" Eventually, incrementally, the dog will be jumping through the hoop.

Rewarding desired behaviors increases the likelihood that they will be repeated. Once a behavior is reliably established as part of an animal's behavioral repertoire, you can then add new, extended behavioral sequences off of those established behaviors. You can thereby "shape" the behavior of animals, including humans, by using positive reinforcement to reward incremental approximations in the direction of a desired final behavior.

Highly manipulative? Yes. But behaviorists would assert that we are being unawarely conditioned by cultural and social reinforcement contingencies all the time anyway, whether we care to admit it or not. So my contention here is that perhaps we can learn how to ethically use the power of positive social reinforcement ("Good job!") to help consciously shape each other's behavior toward a truly sustainable, more equitable, and fulfilling society. It is possible.

Sometimes in our zeal to live in an already transformed society, we tend to overlook, minimize, or invalidate the seemingly inconsequential efforts being made by people all around us. This can backfire. While radical leaps of change (as opposed to slower, incremental reform) are sometimes necessary and called for, it's generally more helpful, when communicating across a divide, to acknowledge and applaud *any and all* incremental changes that move society in a progressive direction.

For example, you might notice that someone who had previously thrown everything in the trash now recycles their newspapers—"Yes!" Applaud them—"Good job!" They may still throw out bottles and plastic, but they have taken a step. Small steps in the right direction can gain momentum and over time add up to a significant change. Criticizing people for not going far enough only tends to discourage further efforts, feed pessimism, and disunite us. Rather than blasting them for not recycling their glass, aluminum, plastic, and so forth, you might *start* with an acknowledgment of their effort to recycle their newspapers—"Alright! Way to go!"

Social acknowledgment can be a powerful form of reward (positive reinforcement) for establishing behaviors of which you'd like to see more.

In a situation like the one above, you might, at a later date, help gradually further shape their behavior by dropping off some information (maybe a pamphlet from a local waste-management service) on how to sort recyclables, and perhaps gift them with an attractive set of bins to make it easier and more enjoyable for them to recycle. They'll likely remember your thoughtfulness every time they throw something out. They'll probably feel good about themselves and their connection with you and also about doing something good for society and the environment. Unlike dogs, people can also derive a sense of pleasure from operating out of a "higher purpose" in life. And it is we humans who have the opportunity at this historic moment to consciously steer the course of global civilization toward a truly wonderful and sustainable future. We are the dominant species on this planet at this time. It is we who hold the power to consciously shape the future. We are capable of rising above our base instincts. We can consciously choose to function at a higher level than fear and greed. We can understand that our survival, as a species, is more likely to result from cooperation than from competition. We can help each other discover and experience our greatest potential by encouraging and applauding each other's acts of courage, cooperation, and compassion according to our highest collective vision.

We can help each other pay attention to what really matters, point out opportunities to do something different about those aspects of the current system that perpetuate the dysfunctions of society, and reward (acknowledge) each other for making positive changes. This will, incrementally, alter the trajectory of the current cultural momentum. As we individually change the ways in which we participate in any system, the system itself is changed. The current socio-economic system is the result of our collective choices and actions to date. Cultural norms evolve as we participate. When we choose to act differently—from a higher purpose and understanding—it becomes easier for others to risk different behavior, also. They don't feel so out of step if they see someone else trying new ways of *being* in society. Successful incremental changes call into question the way society is organized, and whether the current arrangement is the best arrangement we are capable of, or not.

So we can invite each other, support each other, and *reward* each other into taking whatever steps we feel capable of, at any given time, in the direction of progress. We can help each other feel encouraged to show up, speak up, stand up, and be seen as living models of a better interpersonal ethic on the planet. We can avoid letting the irrationality and hopelessness of the current cultural momentums discourage or dissuade us. We can prevent our silence from being misunderstood as condoning the ongoing destruction and exploitation. We can withdraw our participation from those aspects of society that per-petuate harm, while helping shape each other's behavior in more fruitful directions by making it more *rewarding* to do the *right* thing. We can stand in unity with each other, when and where a stand must be taken. We can be alert and pull support from those old structures that fail to meet reasonable human needs and lend our strength to those emerging structures that offer the possibility of a better future for everyone.

Taking a stance beyond business as usual, and being willing to experience and generate a little discomfort in those around us in the process, helps to awaken awareness among *all* that the status quo is not the only way, is not inevitable, and that it *is* possible to question, think, and choose differently. Alternatives *are* possible. A better path forward that includes *all* of us as allies to each other *is* possible. To deny the possibility is to deny the highest aspirations and potential of humanity. With the conscious application of social support as a reward, new behaviors can quickly become cemented into our own and each other's behavioral repertoires. By unashamedly *living* those alternatives that reflect our heartfelt values and highest visions, we model for each other possibilities that otherwise remain hidden or marginalized by mainstream culture. The tension created within the current socio-economic and political systems by our doing this—by the incongruity of our lives, especially to the degree that they are actually more fulfilling than what the dominant culture offers—becomes an incentive toward change for others. After attempts to coerce us back into line, others may eventually become curious and interested in how such alternatives might fit *their* lives.

Small steps rewarded can become new directions—for individuals and for the global community. As powerful and insurmountable as the current cultural momentums seem, they are all, at essence, human created and therefore changeable by humans. Small acts taken by many can arrest and unravel the detrimental aspects of the current system. Large-scale transformational change in beneficial directions is being birthed at this very moment by millions worldwide. Let us encourage and applaud each other's efforts and thereby shape a world in which we want to live.

Grab Bag of Other Ideas

Here are some other ideas and approaches that I've found useful in various situations. Some have been mentioned previously but are explained a little differently or elaborated more fully here.

KNOW THYSELF AND OWN IT

Take the time to figure out your own biases and blind spots. Enlist the assistance of a few clear-thinking, well-informed, compassionate-but-firm friends to help you recognize and acknowledge how your own privileges and conditioning operate in perpetuating aspects of empire that are counter to your espoused values and the forward progress of society. We can all assume that our views are, to some degree, shaped and limited by our placement in the hierarchy of the current global socio-economic system. If you can read this, you've probably had a more fortunate existence than the billions of people who cannot read. It's that basic. Our race, gender, nationality, socio-economic status, physical ability, and so forth, all impact how we see the world around us, what we feel entitled to, and what we tend to focus our attention on.

We need to acknowledge our contribution to the problems we face, and own the fact that the problems of global civilization are *our* problems. This needs to be done in a way that encourages acceptance of responsibility for re-steering our course without getting stuck in feeling guilty, like we're somehow inherently flawed as a species or bad individuals. It's important to take responsibility for changing what needs to be changed without feeling like "it's all our fault." We need to recognize that it's possible to be born into, be conditioned by, and unthinkingly go along with and have our behavior scripted by a socio-economic system that brings about unacceptable consequences—without being a bad person.

The truth is, we participate in ecological destruction simply by living in this society. We consume in order to exist. Yet the options for consumption presented by the current economic system come at great cost to the environment, other species, other people, and future generations. We benefit from the very same system that is destroying our children's prospects for a bountiful future. We must find the courage to stop denying that reality. It does little good to feel guilty or to blame others. And getting bogged down in expert debates, or tussles over controversial issues, only diverts attention and energy away from taking effective action toward collectively conceived solutions.

We can instead strive to understand how our own habits and patterns of living and relating contribute to and perpetuate the interlocking systems of exploitation and degradation, and then make the effort to change them. We can strive to not just become aware of these issues, but to *remain* aware of them in our social interactions and consumer choices throughout our day. This can sometimes be difficult, especially when we feel worn down by the constant time pressures, economic worries, and increasing complexity of modern life. The cultural trance obscures the clarity of our understanding. We exist in a socio-economic system that places profit over people, and profit over a sustainable society. The current cultural momentum defines us and values us, primarily, as consumers and producers of economic productivity. We are confronted, daily, with a massive onslaught of consumer choices and advertising messages that divert us from critical thinking. Maintaining awareness of these issues requires effort and support. We need to be alert, stay alert, and connect with other people who are also paying attention to these issues and are not numbed out. We need to unite our understandings of how the social systems we participate in—family, workplace, community, nation—both define and thereby limit us, and are shaped by our participation in them. It is with this understanding and awareness in-the-moment that we can take steps to actively change the systems in which we participate by changing our choices.

As conscious agents of social evolution, we must be willing to have others around us be a little uncomfortable with our "unusual" choices. We have to be willing to stand out from the "go along, get along" crowd as being a little different. We have to be willing to be the one that doesn't laugh at the stereotyping joke or accept the sound-bite rationale, the one that points out injustice, or questions the unsustainability of a particular activity or consumer choice. We need to practice breaking the silence and openly *not* participating in those aspects of whatever system we find ourselves currently participating in that perpetuate the exploitation of other people or the degradation of the environment. To do otherwise, to remain silent and unnoticed in our dissent, makes us complicit with the destructive momentums.

The risk, of course, which arouses the anxiety that inhibits us, is that we will be invalidated, dismissed, and excluded from future engagement with a particular social group. That's why it's so important to learn how to communicate effectively across the divides. Our willingness to openly make a different choice, take a different stand, rather than going along with the unspoken expectations (peer pressure) of the group, raises to awareness for all involved, the possibility that other alternatives exist. It helps illuminate the reality that no system is static and that it is, in fact, through our participation, and through our choices, that we co-create the systems of which we are a part. They shape us. We shape them. Understanding this truth, our lives can more easily and effectively become part of the Great Turning toward a new paradigm.

CHANGE THE CHANNEL

Encourage people to unplug from TV and expand their sources of news and information. This will help to broaden their views of what's going on in the world beyond the corporate-sponsored pop-culture media version and will likely lessen their cynicism, apathy, and feelings of powerlessness. Use the "TV Addiction" argument: for many people, watching television fits the criteria for maladaptive dependence. That is, watching television is too often used for escape from distress and meaninglessness, and keeps people from addressing the sources of discontent in their lives with constructive action. Many people, if they are honest, admit that they watch more than they really intend to. Most have unsuccessfully tried to reduce their television watching on more than one occasion and note that other valued aspects of their lives, (e.g., social and/or recreational activities), have been displaced by television watching. And, disturbingly, this behavior continues despite recognition of the problems it causes. These are all signs of addiction. Watching TV to "relax" rather than figuring out why you're anxious, frustrated, or depressed, and then taking steps to change your life, is not much different than any other addiction that temporarily "takes you away" from your problems and then delivers you right back to them the next morning. You might also cite research that demonstrates a correlation between the number of hours of television viewed and the increase of depressive symptoms. A potentially self-defeating, self-reinforcing spiral exists here.

As an alternative, you might encourage people to read more by placing some "not too heavy" articles in their path, with a commitment to follow up and talk about the ideas in them.

Another option is to bring a video program with a progressive view and offer to watch it together and then talk about it after. This approach has its own inherent rewards since, for most people, getting together with others to watch a video and hang out a little after is generally more satisfying than "zoning out" alone in front of commercial television. This can also be done with small groups to great benefit.

Let's face it, pop-culture corporate-sponsored media don't offer a meaningful analysis of world events because it arises from, and has a vested interest in, perpetuating the current economic system which is driven by the goal of profit maximization. Therefore, any programming that seriously challenges the validity or inevitability of the status quo is unlikely to attract corporate sponsors. In order for the current news-and-entertainment conglomerate to function profitably and perpetuate itself, the programming offered must not illuminate issues of privilege and exploitation in a manner which might arouse questioning of how the media are being used to manipulate the populace and maintain the oppression of subgroups in society. Instead, the masses must be distracted and pacified with a steady stream of "interesting diversions" to take one's mind off of one's worries and make it through another day. This mind-numbing programming is complemented by sensationalized news bits that stir up fear and divisiveness by pitting subordinate groups against each other—"If it weren't for those illegal aliens, gays, Jews, Arabs, Chinese, etc., who aren't like us ...." This serves the interests of empire. When people are afraid, they are both more easily led by those who promise security, and more desirous of escape (diversion) to alleviate the discomfort of worry. Commercial television provides plenty of both.

What we all need to do is pay more attention to information that actually leads to an increased understanding of how things *really* work, tracking those issues that *really* affect our lives, and sharing inspiring information and programming with each other that encourages critical thinking and constructive changes of behavior. We need to keep our focus on information that empowers us to take charge of our society so that we can steer it in a direction that actually meets the rational needs of humanity.

IS THAT SO?

Question the myth that people are fundamentally greedy, violent, and irrational by nature. Lightly ask, "Is that so?" Pose the possibility that these sorts of behaviors might be conditioned responses to harsh life circumstances, perpetrated by the struggles of a competitively-based socio-economic system. Challenge the myth that those who are different from us are inferior and should be feared and exploited—"Oh, really?" Challenge the myth that things have always been this way, and that they will always be this way—"Oh? Is that so?" Don't accept the myth that the way things are is inevitable. Challenge the myth that the problems we face as a global civilization are too big, and that we are too small to make any difference. Challenge the myth that if we can't see the changes we are working toward in our lifetime then our efforts are not having any effect.

FIVE-PART IMPULSE-CONTROL TECHNIQUE

Here's a process I've used in therapeutic settings for many years. It lends itself well to less-formal situations where unsustainable behavior might be considered the "focus of treatment." The basic idea is to break the unconscious momentums of those habitual behaviors that perpetuate ecological damage by cultivating a five-step process that interrupts them at the "choice point":

1. STOP the behavior. Whatever is about to happen, just halt and make room for something else to happen. Just stop.

2. BREATHE. Take a breath. And then another. Try to just breathe and relax into whatever sensations are occurring in your body and ride out the impulse to … escape, indulge, act-out, whatever. Generally, the impulse will pass within two to twenty minutes. Ride it out.

3. NOTICE where your thinking goes and what you're feeling as you ride out the impulse to act. Notice what's going on inside of you. What has been stirred up? Without judging it (or yourself), simply make note of it, combining awareness with acceptance and curiosity.

4. THINK. When the impulse to act has subsided enough to allow some room to think, go the next step from simply noticing to actually *thinking* about what you notice. *Think* about what you're feeling. Try to identify and label and understand what's going on. What habitual thought patterns have been reactivated? What old feelings are pressing for self-defeating, impulsive action? And most importantly, think about what it is you are *really* needing and longing for. How is it that you mistakenly believe that this underlying healthy need will be satisfied by a certain compulsive behavior or consumer item? Will it really? What uncomfortable feelings would this impulsive behavior help you avoid in the short term? Use this sort of conscious self-inquiry to help gain understanding and control over self-defeating impulses—submitting them to thinking rather than to action.

5. CHOOSE. Choose differently. Choose newly. Choose connection over isolation. Choose what you know is better rather than giving in to the old, habitual patterns. Choose what is in alignment with your heart-felt values rather than your regressive feelings of the moment. Make the healthier choice.

Following this process and practicing it over time will result in learning how impulsive, self-defeating choices are reinforced by immediate gratification and relief from discomfort. It will also become clear how those same choices ultimately result in long-term suffering, a weakening of confidence, and lowered self-esteem. Healthy choices, on the other hand, strengthen one's self-esteem, sense of personal power, and resolve to pursue a meaningful life. The choice is ours.

BETTER OUT THAN IN

Welcome the expression of frustration and anger in appropriate and growth-promoting ways. Many people are angry about the situation we find ourselves in as a civilization, and they should be. If you're not upset, you're not paying attention. It needs to be OK to vent those feelings in constructive ways so as to not become stuck in despair or apathy. There's a saying in the field of psychology that, "depression is the result of anger turned inward" meaning that generally, it's better to get your angry feelings out (in appropriate ways) than to keep them in. The trick is learning how to harness that potentially explosive volume of energy and directing it into focused, productive social-change efforts. To some degree, in a slightly different way, the same holds true for feelings of sadness and fear. It's possible to find ways to make it safe to feel them, express them, and channel them into productive action.

EVER-CHANGING SYSTEMS

Societies are fluid, dynamic, constantly changing. While they may *appear* to be solid, stationary, monolithic structures, they are really never static. Societies are the result of the myriad social interactions among the human beings that make up that particular system. Societies arise and change as people participate in their daily lives. Societies are constantly reshaping themselves. They are the manifest outcome of our individual and collective choices, never the same as they were, and will never be tomorrow what they are today. That's important to understand. Systems continue to evolve whether we like it or not.

Some systems *seem* more stable than others, especially those that limit people's options and suppress their aspirations so much that it's difficult for them to imagine other possibilities—especially if people can't remember a time when it wasn't that way. How we find ourselves organized as a society can easily be mistaken for "normal" or "inevitable."

But no form of social organization lasts forever. All societies, all groups, are constantly changing. Seemingly stable organizational structures come and go. Their apparent stability is only an illusion. It's hard to know how they will change, and whether what they change into will be better or worse. Some changes happen more rapidly. Some changes seem to take forever. Nonetheless, all societies change over time. They *will* change, and they *are* changing at this very moment. It's only a question of how quickly or slowly, by what means, and toward what alternatives. I think it can be useful to remind each other of this, as it can help us to feel less stuck with unsatisfying circumstances and trajectories as a civilization. The general trend of humanity seems to be toward the continual birthing of new social structures that are better than the ones left behind. It is the contention of this author that intelligently striving for progressive change that both honors basic human needs and supports the fulfillment of humanity's greatest potential is a worthwhile endeavor for a meaningful life.

ZOOM OUT

Zoom back. Strive for a broader, higher, longer view of things. Expand your consciousness to embrace a picture of reality that is beyond your own limited individual life. Step back and look at yourself, and your life. Then stretch your view beyond yourself and beyond your personal reference groups— beyond your friends, family, co-workers, and so forth. Keep going, keep expanding your awareness beyond your local community, state, and nation, beyond your lifespan, beyond your species, beyond your planet. From out here, take a look back at the earth. Notice how small and malleable those seemingly overwhelming societal structures and institutions seem from this vantage point. We can help facilitate this shift of consciousness—from identification with the individual ego perspective to identification with a higher, broader vantage point—by reminding each other that it is *possible* to take a bigger view. This makes it easier for all of us to unhook from our defensive positions with each other, to let go of rigidly held views and consider other possibilities, to see how arbitrary and changeable all human societies are. A broader view also tends to lessen anxiety and loosen the tightness and sense of urgency around having to take care of it all *right now*. From this more relaxed, spacious perspective, separation seems ever-more-clearly an illusion, and different points of view seem like just that—different views of the same one undivided reality. We are entering an age of extreme paradoxes where both the best and the worst of humanity will be manifesting simultaneously before our eyes. We will witness and experience incredibly wonderful breakthroughs and gestures of compassion and generosity simultaneously with hideous atrocities and disasters. Suffering will accrue around the either/or dualistic clashes that ensue, while those who are able to adopt a more "enlightened" and integrated view will be better situated, psychologically, to see possible paths forward that embrace the whole.

WOO-WOO SECRET

Without drifting off into New-Age magical thinking, consider that it is sometimes helpful to assume the possibility that our thoughts and beliefs do somehow seem to manifest themselves in reality. Without getting caught up in trying to understand or explain the mechanisms involved, and without getting into a debate about the scientific proof of (or lack thereof) such a phenomenon, try to just recognize that the notion of "self-fulfilling prophecy" is one that most people seem to grasp intuitively. Perhaps imagining other possibilities, other possible alternative futures, in-and-of-itself might have some value, in that it tends to loosen our grasp on otherwise rigidly held ideas about how things *are* and *must* be. How about imagining a global community that is materially sufficient, more economically equitable, ecologically sustainable, and more emotionally, socially, and spiritually fulfilling than our current paradigm? Imagine.

PLANT TREES

It's important to understand that if we want to participate in large-scale, evolutionary social change, we must not limit ourselves to conceptions and actions measured by our single human life span. This tends to stifle us from thinking big and long-term. Progress on a grander scale requires us to consider the longer arc of historical progress and to find, accept, and honor our place in that upward march. We need to relate to time differently, and to recognize that we can contribute to significant changes whether we are around to see them or not. Civilization thrives when elders plant trees.

HOPE

Promote hope by focusing attention and energy on building the new emerging culture, rather than getting caught up in futilely fighting against a corrupt, broken system. Invite others to join into an upwelling of unity with diversity (community) where abundance (enough, plenty) and fun (synergy) prevail. Don't underestimate what we're capable of achieving in the long run. Everything is possible.

AHHH, THE GREAT OUTDOORS

Science is beginning to quantify the restorative benefits of nature. Apparently, we should all be spending more time outside listening to the silence.

Part One

Why The Book?

The current cultural momentum is:

- unsustainable
- unsatisfying
- conditioned
- fear and greed based
- changeable, but...

- Personal Growth
- Moral Maturity
- Social Evolution
- Human Potential

Part Two

Three Things

Understand the person you are talking with:

- **Section One**
  their unique
  CHARACTER STYLE

- **Section Two**
  their
  CURRENT WORLDVIEW

- **Section Three**
  which
  EXISTENTIAL CONCERN
  they are struggling with

Part Three

Techniques

You might try:

- listening
- "between the lines"
- parallel their arguments
- question assumptions
- change the context
- stick to common ground
- applaud all steps
- other ideas...

Part Four

Examples

Imagine yourself in:

- An Awkward Event

- A Workplace Conflict

- Air Travel Delay

Examples Of
Difficult Conversations

10 Examples Of Difficult Conversations

Introduction

I'D LIKE TO START THIS SECTION BY REITERATING MY DISCLAIMER THAT I'M
not very good at this. Like all of us, my characterological defensiveness gets
triggered by what people say and I find myself responding in an unkind manner. When my existential anxieties are aroused by talking about the challenges
that lie ahead, my eyes glaze over and my thinking grinds to a halt. I can't, for
the life of me, remember what might be helpful or hopeful to say. And, being
human, my worldview taints, distorts, and limits everything I see, hear, and say.

Nonetheless, these are important issues that require our best collective
thinking in order to achieve the best possible outcome for humanity, and so
I persist. It's also been my observation that talking across the divides in our
everyday lives about these important issues is not difficult just for me, but for
an increasing number of people in recent years. This concerns me and thus
I have written this book—my attempt to bring together, in one place, some
of the understandings and techniques that I have found helpful.

I will obviously not attempt to present examples representing every combination of character style, worldview, underlying anxiety, and technique. There
are too many possibilities and, as mentioned before, the categorizations used
in this book are, of necessity, crude generalizations about the myriad mix-
tures and blends that make up *real* people.

It's also important to keep in mind that the examples presented here are
composite creations and should be viewed as nothing more than one-of-
many possible ways of thinking about and responding to a hypothetical
situation (and not necessarily the best way). They should not be followed or
parroted as gospel. Real-life situations require that you tailor your approach
to account for *your* particular way of thinking, *your* character type, *your*
worldview, as well as the unique situation, topic, and person with whom you
are dealing—*at that moment.* I am simply presenting a *process* that I have
found helpful, at times, in hopes that you might find something of value to
add to your own evolving repertoire of wisdom in these matters.

The process presented here is somewhat similar to how a clinician might arrive at a dynamic formulation or make a diagnostic assessment. That is —listen closely and respectfully, ask questions, listen some more, and try (in your mind) different ways of juxtaposing the pieces of information coming at you until they seem to coalesce into a coherent, recognizable pattern. Then, formulate some hypotheses and begin testing them. If "x" is true, then "y" should become apparent if I say .... As you verify the *character type* of person with whom you are talking, their *worldview*, and the *sources of anxiety* that are presently stimulated, you can then try tailoring your responses using the techniques listed previously (and/or others of your own) in a strategic effort to communicate more effectively.

Please note that brackets like [this] will be used to indicate what your internal thought process (your "self-talk") might be as the dialogue unfolds.

An Awkward Social Event

YOU'VE BEEN INVITED BY A SENIOR CO-WORKER TO ATTEND A PARTY AT HER house on Saturday afternoon. You were hoping to get your laundry done and catch up with your personal e-mail. Or maybe sit on the back porch and stare at your tomato plants for an hour while the frenetic energy of the work-week settles. But Mary's been really supportive of you at work, and you want to reciprocate her kindness.

Finding your way through the twisty, hilly, newer neighborhood she lives in has you feeling a bit nervous. Something about it feels like a gated community.

[McMansions. Plywood castles. Immaculate landscaping—like a park. Why aren't there any people outside? How is it that all of these new houses look so similar, when they're all trying to appear so unique? What planet is this?]

You find a place to park and walk up the white cement walkway that crosses a huge, bright-green, half-inch, crew-cut lawn that doesn't have a single sprig of clover or hint of dandelion or other broadleaf life form.

[A dynamic biological process held in a static state of limbo by chemicals and machinery.]

The steps to the front door are wide enough for eighteen people across.

[I'll bet my little brother and his friends would love to skateboard on this.]

Approaching the front door.

[Hmm. I wonder if there will be *anyone* here I can relate to—somebody to hang out with who shares my cynical sense of humor and irreverent views of world events. I like Mary, she's got great energy at work and feels like an ally—even if she is old enough to be my mother. But judging by this neighborhood and all the SUVs ... I don't know ... all the subtle pretense and competition ... I really hate making small talk and being "pleasant" when things are falling apart all around us. Of course, it probably doesn't affect these people at all. Oh well, there's probably going to be plenty of food, even if none of it is local, seasonal, or organic. Okay, here goes ...]

Ding-Dong-Dung-Dooong, ooong, ooong, ooong, ooong.

[Wow, what a doorbell.]

Mary: (excitedly) *"Hi! Welcome. It's so good to see you. I'm so glad you were able to make it after all. Come on in."*

You: *"Hi Mary."* You step through one of the two four-foot wide, ten-foot high, solid-oak doors, looking cautiously through the spacious entrance hall, that has about a dozen people in it holding drinks, across into the great room where there appears to be about sixty more people.

[Oh my God, I'm not dressed for this. Hey, is that Wilson over by the food table?]

Mary: (immediately directing your attention to the closest person) *"This is my neighbor Jonathan Charles Broadworth. He's director of the academy at the country club and owner of the new airport complex—you know, the new hotel and restaurant plaza with all those neat little shops?"*

You: *"Uh, yeh. I mean, yes, sure. The place with all the flags and fountains and ..."*

[The place my friends and I protested because of the paving over of local wetlands.]

He reaches out a hand and politely bows his head a few inches while staring squarely into your eyes with a polished smile and giving you a well-rehearsed greeting and firm-but-friendly handshake.

J. Charles: *"Just call me J. Charles."*

You: *"It's nice to meet you."*

[Whoa. Check out those gold accessories. I'll bet this guy doesn't worry about paying the rent on time.]

J. Charles: *"What do you do?"*

[Oh, great. Here we go. Do? What *do* I do? Why do I always freeze up when people ask me this? How do I justify my existence to a guy like this. Alright, focus. What do I do? Hey, wait a minute. This guy probably isn't really interested in who I am. Not really. Probably just angling to see if my great uncle has a piece of real estate that he might be able to exploit. Alright, stop it. Don't be cynical. Give the guy a chance.]

Mary: (politely stepping away and turning her attention to another guest coming through the front door) *"Excuse me."*

You: *"Uh … I work at the non-profit with Mary."*

J. Charles: *"Oh, I see. What do you do there?"*

You: *"Uh … I'm just an intern, but hoping maybe a position will open up if I hang around long enough."*

J. Charles: *"And so you … "*

You: *"I'm, uh, interested in economic theory and social justice."*

[Oh crap. Why'd I say that? This is not the guy to talk with about that stuff. Not at Mary's party.]

J. Charles: *"Economics? Fascinating. Do say more."*

You: *"Oh, I just mean, uh … I think it's fascinating, yes, fascinating, how our economic system works."*

J. Charles: *"Oh? Well, it seems we have something in common. It's really quite a marvel, isn't it? This economic system of ours. With all of the opportunities and endless, upward potential for everyone. I find it truly amazing. Such prosperity."*

You: *"Uh, yeh. Life is good. Lots of potential. I mean, there's lots of different possibilities … for, uh, how we might all live together and get along, and, uh, you know, different ways we might try living as a society."*

[What did I just say? God, that was really lame. Alright, focus. Think. Engage this guy. No. No. Escape. Look for a graceful exit. Do I know anybody here? Stop. Focus. Think. Listen. Yes, listen. Try just listening.]

J. Charles: *"Oh? Yes, I guess there have been a number of ill-guided attempts to do things differently throughout the course of history. Miserable failures, of course. All of them. How incredible for us, though, to be living at this historic time when it's so easy to generate endless wealth on a global scale. Helping poor people around the world to join the rest of us in the pleasures of life. Extraordinary, don't* *you think? I find it puzzling that anyone could be financially challenged in an economic system such as this. Don't you?"*

You: *"Oh, um. I don't know. How do you mean?"*

[Good. Keep him talking. Just listen. I'm sure he'll have no problem pontificating from his privileged perch. Stop it. Be nice. Smile. Warmly, not stiffly.]

J. Charles: *"I mean it's so easy to better one's circumstances and accumulate wealth in this economic system of ours that a person has to be lazy, or just plain stupid, to not cash in on the incredible deals that abound. Why just this week my accountant told me I raked in over $14,000 from stock options—and I didn't have to lift a finger. Can you imagine? Who can't make money doing that?"*

[Careful. Don't react. Go slowly. Keep smiling and listening. Think. Think.]

You: *"Uh, well, a lot of people, I guess."*

J. Charles: *"Well, like I said. Some people just don't have it. They just don't see the opportunities in front of their noses or are not motivated enough to grab for them."*

[Boy, this guy seems incredibly out of touch with how hard it is for most people to make a living. He comes off as thinking he's so much better than everybody else. Probably a Self-Important character style—on the narcissistic end of the spectrum. Definitely an Industrious-Achievement worldview—looking to exploit every possible situation for personal gain. I'll bet he's spent most of his life in a hurry, chasing after material success and trying to impress other people with how important he is. Probably feels pretty empty inside. Probably doesn't have many real friends or even know how to just sit and relax and enjoy himself without a glass of wine to numb his feelings and the TV on for distraction. Probably hasn't taken much time to reflect on how hollow all of those achievements really are and how meaningless they will seem at the end of his life. I think I'll try listening for these things and see what happens.]

J. Charles: *"You know, if people would just understand the way capitalism really works—that it is possible for us to continually grow new markets and sell each other more and more of whatever it is that brings us pleasure. And that by doing this, we help each other, and society, to enjoy greater and greater wealth on an* *endless, upward ascent. This is the power of the free market system. If we can just keep taxes low and regulations out of the way, and get people off welfare and onto a payroll somewhere, then the naturally competitive feelings between us will deliver the best of what life has to offer at the cheapest possible price—and we all benefit. It's so simple. Surely you agree."*

[Sheesh. I don't think it's gonna be possible, in a few short minutes at this party, to really move this guy's thinking very much about the *im*possibility of infinite growth on a finite planet. He's not even close to recognizing that there are real, physical-biological limits to constantly increasing the material and energy throughputs for the billions of people who are just now reaching the consumer class. And his justifications are probably bullet-proof around ideas of deregulation and privatization being the best path forward for civilization. Confronting his self-important arrogance by going after his belief that unrestrained self-interest (greed) is what allows the "invisible hand" of the market to fill every basket—that selfishly and aggressively pursuing personal gain is ultimately the best for everyone—would probably only stimulate defensiveness. He doesn't seem to understand the Standard of Living versus Quality of Life equation. Maybe I'll try approaching that. It might resonate with his unsatisfied inner core.]

You: *"Uh, I don't know. I've read some studies that show that continually increasing wealth is not necessarily correlated with greater happiness—beyond a certain point, you know. And I guess some people choose to be happier in life."*

[That was a little oblique to where he was heading, but not too bad.]

J. Charles: *"Oh? What could make a person happier than being rich?"*

You: *"Well, I don't know for sure. I mean, I guess it's really an individual thing, but I think there is a distinction to be made between a person's 'quality of life,' and their 'standard of living.' I mean, having enough is important. But beyond a certain point, I guess having more doesn't necessarily make one happier. At least that's what these studies show."*

J. Charles: *"Well, I'd be very interested in seeing those studies sometime."*

You: *"Yes, well, they're pretty easy to find on the internet. And they're really pretty interesting. Try Googling 'quality of life indicators.'"*

J. Charles: *"Indicators? Well, yes, I mean what you say has some merit. Why I know a number of people with great wealth whose happiness is what you might call ... deficient."*

[Is he talking about other people? Or about himself? Listen closely. And smile.]

You: *"Deficient?"*

J. Charles: *"Well ... not as happy as they wish they were ... as they should be. You know, these are people capable of accomplishing anything they set their minds to. People whose assets buy them the finest that life has to offer. And yet ... happiness somehow eludes them. Sad, in an ironic sort of way, wouldn't you say?"*

You: *"Unfortunate, yes. I wonder what might be missing for such individuals. I mean, what are they really wanting that they don't have?"*

J. Charles: *"Well that, of course, is the key question. When a person has everything, what can possibly be missing? I guess sometimes it seems that we have such a short amount of time to leave our mark on life and to consume its pleasures, that ... well, we needn't go there."*

[Sounds like he's running into an awareness of the impermanence of life. Maybe I can test this hypothesis by gently steering him in that direction.]

You: *"Oh, please do go on. Short amount of time to leave one's mark? I'm very interested in hearing your views about this. I think this is really important and must be one of the great universal struggles of humanity."*

J. Charles: (flattered) *"Really? Well, as I was saying..."*

It becomes apparent, as he continues, that he is (indirectly) talking about himself and that the existential anxiety he is wrestling with has to do with no longer existing (death) and the impermanence of everything he has spent his life chasing after. He is quick to use denial ("We needn't go there") and lots of paid cultural diversions (e.g., travel, entertainment, fine wine, etc.) to avoid feeling hopeless and futile. And, in typical counter-depressive fashion, spends his "productive" hours manically working to create monuments (e.g., the airport complex) by which he might "live on" indefinitely. Your warm validations and empathetic stance about how hard it is to realize that everything one achieves must be left behind, allows him to relax his formality a little.

He reveals how the relentless passage of years has made him aware of the inevitability of decline and eventual death, and how his legacy has become increasingly important.

[Legacy might be a good segue to sustainability.]

You: *"Yes. Our legacy is all we have to be remembered by. I wonder, sometimes, what future generations will think about us. Will they think of us as wise and generous for having considered them in the choices we are making today? Will they have a chance at as good a life as we've had?"*

[Or will they spit on our graves because we selfishly squandered the bounty of resources we inherited on our own short-term pleasure and left them a polluted mess to clean up?]

J. Charles: *"Well, you know, that makes me think about something. One of the architect's assistants at the design charrette we had for the airport complex kept talking about sustainable this and sustainable that. And really, I found it annoying at first, and had little interest unless it offered some sort of economic advantage—you know, efficiency and all of that. But the guy kept pushing and presenting ideas. I think in the end, we settled for some sort of certification scheme, LEEDS I think they called it. They all seemed pleased. The accountants assured me that the numbers worked out in our favor, and the property management staff thought it might be good for public relations, so I went along."*

[This is a great opportunity to stroke his ego, which he'll probably sop up, and applaud his steps in the direction of sustainability, which will hopefully encourage more of this behavior.]

You: *"Yes, I've heard of LEEDS. It's a well-known leading-edge certification program. Your decision in this matter makes you one of the bold pioneers in an emerging field. That's something you can feel really proud of. And those sustainable design elements assure that your project will live on and be cherished by future generations as a magnanimous effort. Good for you."*

J. Charles: *"Well thank you. Thank you. I mean it. Thank you. It feels good to be acknowledged for trying new things. I think maybe I'll look more into this sort of thing."*

You: *"Yes."*

[I suspect that without a *lot* of learning and personal growth on his part, that he's probably, really, less interested in doing something good for humanity than in realizing a profit and status for himself. Maybe I can keep some momentum going and steer him toward the alternative energy boom as the "next big thing" and a good prospect for success. This probably has more appeal to his current level of consciousness than the idea of collective future well-being.]

You: *"You know, by the way, I hear there's a lot of growth potential for investors in the wind power sector these days. A person with your means might be able to really capitalize on such a situation. I can see it now—the Broadworth Wind Farm: providing renewable energy for society's needs, now and for the future."*

A deep silence falls between you and a warm feeling of connection occurs. Your words have created a pause in time. The distant look in his eyes tells you he's entranced in your vision of a possible future that he hadn't ever considered before.

J. Charles: (gently arriving back at present time) *"Hmm. Interesting. Well, I do hope maybe you'll come by the complex and see me some time. I'd like to show you around."*

You: *"I definitely will. It's been really nice talking with you J. Charles."*

J. Charles: *"Please. Just call me J."*

You: *"Alright, J."*

You: (in an upbeat tone that begins the break away) *"Say, I'm kinda hungry. I think maybe I'll go over to ..."*

J. Charles: (taking your cue and responding in upbeat fashion) *"Oh, by all means, please do."* (bowing his head a few inches as he holds out his hand for a warm, farewell handshake) *"It's been an absolute pleasure."*

You walk through the entrance hall into the great room toward the food table.

[Damn, that's not Wilson. What the heck? Are those strawberries? They're as big as baseballs. Some sort of science specimens.]

You pick up a fist-sized strawberry off a polished silver platter and take a bite.

[Hmm. Gigantic. Off-season. Tough and mealy. Flavorless. What a pathetic example of our current food system.]

Fade to black....

A Workplace Conflict

YOU'VE BEEN WORKING AT THE SAME INDUSTRIAL PLANT FOR ALMOST SEVEN-teen years now. It's been OK. Hard physical work, but a steady paycheck and mostly fair. You've worked with a lot of people over the years and gotten to know a few of them pretty well. Most seem like just ordinary decent folks—just trying to get through life without any major calamities. But there's also been a "keep your head down and stay in line" atmosphere since management went through all that upheaval about rising healthcare costs a few years ago. A lot of people were unhappy about the changes. And manage-ment's response wasn't exactly appreciated by those who got the short end of the stick. There's still a fair amount of unresolved tension around the plant. Recently, management has taken steps to discourage any attempts by line workers, like yourself, to organize for better benefits. They've even unofficially enlisted and elevated a few tough-guy informers from the line to keep an eye on the floor.

You're on your twenty-minute afternoon break in the staff room. You brought a handful of half-page announcements for an after-hours meeting at the local pub next month. A few of you have been talking about approaching management with a new proposal. You're standing by the staff bulletin board getting ready to post a copy of the announcement when you spot a co-worker heading your way from across the room.

[Oh, great. Here comes Rick and his goons. Management's enforcement squad.]

Rick, a squarely built, strong, capable worker who's been here a few months longer than you, hones in on you from the far doorway of the breakroom. He walks briskly, diagonally across the room, never taking his eyes off of you. He pushes past people, around chairs and tables, leading with his chin. He picks up speed, obviously coming directly for you like a predator closing in on prey and steps right in between you and the bulletin board. Standing a little too close, his face looming large in yours, with his chest *almost* touching yours, he looks you square in the eye.

[Man, I never really noticed how massive this guy's jaw is before. Looks like he hasn't shaven in three days.]

Rick: *"What's up Johnson? What'dya got there?"*

Trying to stand tall and square-on to him without flinching or blinking, summoning up your best, calm, confident voice, you hold one of the announcements up for him to see.

You: *"Hi Rick. Oh, just an announcement about an upcoming..."*

Rick: *"Didya run that past Frank?"*

You: *"Uh ... no, but I thought the policy was..."*

He grabs it out of your hand.

Rick: *"Lemme see that."*

Glances at it without reading it.

Rick: *"Nothing goes on the board or tables without Frank's clearance. Got it?"*

You: *"Uh, yeah. But I thought..."*

Rick: *"Don't think so much, Johnson. Just do your job. Just do what you're told."*

He turns away dismissively and walks toward the door with his entourage following in lockstep behind him, leaving you stunned, intimidated. You finally exhale and move your neck a little to dislodge the numbness.

[Hmm. O.K. Well, then. Let's see.]

You spot an ally, Bob, and a few other co-workers digging through brown paperbags for sandwich ends and pepperoni sticks at a table across the room. You unlock your knees and begin to slowly walk toward them. Finally breathing normally again, you sit down at their table. Their down-turned eyes and silence make it clear that they know what just happened. They've seen it before.

Bob: *"So ... how'd that go, Johnson?"*

You: *"Uh, well ... you know ... I think Rick ... uh ... just wants to make sure that management doesn't ... uh ... Damn! Ya know what? After hours ... off grounds ... it's really none of their business."*

Bob: *"Oh? I don't know about that. These walls have ears. And if management catches on to anything they don't like, you'll be lucky if you just lose your job."*

You: *"Yeh, I know, but HR said the breakroom bulletin board was…"*

Bob: *"Doesn't matter. You know what happened to Drysdale last year. Maybe it's not worth it. Maybe we should just…"*

You: *"Oh, crimony. I know! But it's just not right. We can't just…"*

Bob: *"Johnson … lemme tell you something."*

Bob goes on to warn you about the possible consequences of arousing management's scrutiny, and to be especially careful to *not* cross swords with Rick.

You know Rick. And you know that Rick is nobody to mess with. You know that challenging him in front of others would be a *big* mistake. But you also know that underneath all of that toughness, he's just a person, just another line worker like you who's being stepped on by management—again. You also know that in his personal life he's had a hard go of it. From the bits you've pieced together over the years, you know that he had a pretty unstable childhood in a rough, lower-class part of town. Divorced parents, moved a lot, a series of uncaring, hard-drinking stepfathers, domestic violence. You feel sorry for him. He's had to look out for himself since he was just a kid. In some ways, that tough exterior is understandable. It's kept him alive. But you also know that while he's tough on the outside, he's also very lonely and a good person underneath all that "I don't need anybody" armor. Kind of like a mistreated animal that's ready to lash out to defend itself, but really it just wants a safe place to rest and be fed.

You remember back when you first started working at the plant, you and Rick worked together for several years on the same shift and project team. You were both a lot younger then and seemed to get along just fine. There was mutual respect and even some sense of camaraderie as lowly beginners together. In fact, you went fishing a few times on weekends, before life became so complicated for you both. Those were good times.

Then Rick got his girlfriend pregnant. He was only nineteen years old. The poor guy was married with three kids and in over his head before he knew what was happening. By the time he was twenty-three he was already going through an ugly and expensive divorce with a lot of legal complications. He served some jail time for abusive behavior—breaking a restraining order and resisting arrest. He lost everything and has paid dearly ever since. The plant took him back because he's such a strong worker and because the other men naturally follow his lead. But he's been pretty much a lone wolf since his divorce. Hangs out in the bars. Never brings a woman-friend to company picnics or holiday celebrations. You've heard that even his kids want nothing to do with him. Sad, really. Because underneath, you know that has to hurt.

You know he's capable of feeling and caring. You've seen it under severe working conditions more than once when he's been the one to take charge and jump in when others hesitate—right into the middle of the most dangerous, dirty part of a job where a co-worker's error has put everyone at risk. Rick's been the one to save the situation, rescue a co-worker's reputation, and keep the plant from suffering an expensive setback. His silence afterwards attests to his underlying character and goodwill. Never asking for thanks or seeking praise. Never chiding the man who erred. He's a quiet hero, respected by the other men, in this regard.

Yet lately, he's not just respected by the other men—he's also *feared*. Much more so since management began using him to keep an eye on the other line workers. He's definitely scary when he gets mad. Not afraid of anything, and quick to escalate. He would never back down from a fight and every-one knows it. Human Resources has had to send him to anger management classes more that once for incidents with co-workers. No one has been seriously injured, but more than one worker has been seriously rattled by the collisions.

It appears to you that management is encouraging this "tough guy" aspect of his personality to further their own interests. They look the other way so as to not appear complicit with his intimidating style. But they use him, nonetheless, to gain compliance with their unpopular policies. He must seem like an easy bribe to them. Just give him the *illusion* of affiliation ("You're one of us") and a few inconsequential perks—like extra tickets to a ball game and a preferred parking place in the company lot—and he'll do what he's told. In some ways, this new role he's playing for management probably feels pretty good. He gets to be the one who is in charge instead of the one being stepped on by life.

You decide to pursue the matter directly with Rick—trusting that you can reach the person underneath that role he's currently playing. You turn to Bob.

You: *"I'm gonna have a talk with Rick."*

Bob drops his gaze and shakes his head as if to imply that you are hopeless, that the situation is hopeless, that what you're doing is self-defeating, suicidal. The other guys at the table clear their throats and begin to stand up and head back to their workstations, also shaking their heads. Bob turns a little toward you, raises his head and looks you in the eye.

Bob: *"OK, Johnson. You win. But, watch yourself."*

The next day you arrive at the plant early and ask your immediate supervisor if you can take off for lunch a few minutes early today. He says, fine.

Ten minutes before the lunch whistle, you shut down your workstation and head for Rick's area hoping to catch him before he's surrounded by his henchmen. You know better than to try talking with him in front of others. You also know that he's likely to respect strength, reason, and an opportunity for personal gain.

As you approach Rick's workstation, you're aware that he doesn't notice you walking toward him. You don't want to surprise him from behind, so you walk into his side peripheral vision. You try to ground yourself—relaxed and confident, with a smile. He glances sideways and sees you, spins and turns immediately to face you straight on with a bit of a glare, standing tall and ready for whatever happens next.

You: *"Hi Rick. Say, I was wondering if I could ask you something."*

He stands still and cold and solid as a stone, not responding.

You: *"I was wondering if you'd be willing to meet with me—just you and me—at the pub after work some time this week."*

He stares deeply into your eyes looking for any indication of insincerity, challenge, or weakness.

Rick: (after a long pause) *"What're you up to, Johnson?"*

You: *"Oh, I just wanted a chance for you and me, one-on-one, to talk about some things."*

Rick: *"What things?"*

You: *"Oh, several things. More than I really want to get into here."*

A long silence falls between you. He looks you up and down, confirming in his own mind that he can easily kick your ass—and two of your friends at the same time—if you try anything.

Rick: *"One-on-one?"*

You: *"Yeah."*

Rick: *"Sure. Let's do it."*

You: *"Great. When would be a good day?"*

Rick: *"Today."*

You: *"Uh … great. All right. How about I'll just plan to see you at the pub after work? Just you and me."*

He looks at you suspiciously, eyes narrowed, looking again for any hint of deception or malintent. He nods slowly and ever so slightly, signaling that he'll be there.

After hours at the pub. You have gone directly from work to be sure you got a booth that offers some privacy.

Rick arrives a few minutes later. He spots you immediately upon entering, but then takes his time in the doorway, before walking across the room to your table, to check out who's there and what he might be up against. He nods to a few people who notice him enter. As he approaches your table you reach up to shake hands, aware that your hand is a little cold and sweaty.

You: *"Hi, Rick. Thanks for coming. Have a seat."*

Your hand is dangling in space as he looks around the immediate tables and booths making a final check on who is where before sitting down. Then he finally shakes your hand, looking you right in the eye—dead serious—before sitting down across from you. He pushes his silverware and napkin aside, so that there is nothing between you.

Rick: *"What's up, Johnson?"*

You: *"Rick, really, thanks for coming to talk with me for a few minutes. I really appreciate it."*

Rick: *"Get on with it, Johnson."*

You: *"Well, I uh, wanted to talk about a couple of things. One is, as you know, a lot of guys at the plant are still very unhappy about the changes in our health-care benefits. And you heard, I'm sure, how that change affected Wilson's family. And you know about Charlie with his bad back. Well, some of us were thinking that...."*

You go on to spell out how the changes are not only unfair but how it's hurting the lives of people he knows, and isn't even really a good long-term financial policy for the company—people put off getting the treatment they need until their medical conditions worsen and it ends up costing the company even more.

Rick: *"So? What does this have to do with* me?*"*

[OK. Go slowly. Don't "lock horns" with him. Try to get him to see that we're on the same side, that he has the same classification level as you—not management—and reason with him that the policy is not fair to *him*. Suggest that he might be able to be a key player as the interface between management and classified employees, gaining even more power, more legitimacy and influence if this is approached thoughtfully.]

You: *"Well, I was thinking that maybe you, along with me if you like, or maybe by yourself if you think that would be better, could help explain to Frank and some of the other guys in management, how it's not really a good thing for the company. You know Frank really respects you. And so do I. And so do the other men on the line. You could be a key player in making things better for everybody."*

Rick: *"You've got the wrong guy, Johnson. That's not my thing."*

[Oops, that's right. He's probably less interested in making things better for everyone else than getting *his* share of the pie. Nobody watched out for him when he was young, so he's not really watching out for anyone but himself. Stick with how it will benefit *him* directly.]

You: *"You know, Rick. What we're asking for isn't anything wrong. And the meetings at the pub are just to give us all a chance to hear each other's thoughts about it. I mean, let's face it, those guys in management are getting paid much more than us, and they're also getting much better benefit packages. And those of us who are doing the really hard work are not only getting paid much less, but now we have less healthcare coverage, less employer contribution to the plan, and higher co-pays at the doctor's office. And that includes you Rick. That affects you."*

Rick: *"Look Johnson. The system is unfair. It's always been that way, and it's always gonna be that way. You've gotta stop trying to stir up trouble and just accept your place and deal with it."*

[Hmmm. The inevitability argument. His life has been filled with unfairness and discouragement and hopelessness. And unfortunately, his interpersonal style can be so brusque and scary that it leaves him pretty isolated socially. He's gotta be very lonely. Try staying with that. Stay with your connection to him, one-to-one, at this very moment, and try to help him feel safe and appreciated. Help him relax his vigilance and feel like his back is covered, like you're looking out for him, too. And start by agreeing.]

You: *"You're right, Rick. Yes. There is a pecking order. It is better to be higher up rather than the one being stepped on. I agree. I hear what you're saying. And I'm not saying that things haven't been this way for a long time. But I don't believe that just because something has been a certain way, means that it always has to be that way. I mean, look at how our talks with management seven or eight years ago led to those safety regs that we use every day now. It's been a good thing for us. For you and me. There've been a lot fewer injuries on the floor. You know that. And that's a good thing. For you and me and the company. That's all I'm looking for. Now I'm not saying that I can guarantee anything, but maybe if we approach this thing right, maybe we can get management to recognize that we have enough people interested in further negotiations that it will help everybody, including the company."*

[Man, if I could just get him to stand up for our side on this issue. What an asset he would be. He could stare down anybody in management.]

For the sake of brevity, let's say that by this point, you took some time to think about and craft a rational statement of your position, and that you have made your case compellingly enough—without a whiny tone and without challenging Rick's need to feel dominant and without promising anything you can't deliver—that he sees some possibility of compromise and personal gain by considering your position.

Rick: *"Look, Johnson. You and I have had no problems in the past. But Frank has been pretty good to me. He let me lead on the Anderson project and said that maybe, if things go well, a few years down the road, he might be able to put in a good word for me, and ... you know, he took me out to lunch a few months ago and gave me tickets to the ball game, and ... I really don't want to let him down or blow my chance at getting a step up outta this shit-hole life I've been stuck in. This is my shot and I'm not gonna let anybody take it away from me, you under-stand? I've never got any breaks before and I don't wanna blow it."*

[Validate his self-interest and aspirations to better his circumstances.]

You: *"I understand, Rick. Honestly. And I would never do anything to jeopardize your chances of advancement. You're a good man and a good worker and I respect you a lot. I'm in your corner and I'll also put in a good word for you any time I can. All I'm asking at this point is that you* think *about what I'm saying.* Think *about whether there might be a way to impress Frank and the others with your leadership skills. The men look up to you. And I think you could be a great asset to the company by being the in-between guy, between management and lineworkers. That would give you real credibility on both sides."*

A long silence. You can see he's thinking about it. His face looks a little more relaxed, but his body is starting to stir.

Rick: *"All right Johnson. I'll think about it."*

You: *"Great. That's all I'm asking. Oh, and yeah, Rick, the other thing I wanted to talk about is, you know the salmon are gonna be running up river here in a few weeks and I thought maybe, you know, we haven't been fishing together in a long time, and maybe you'd like to take a day and go hammer some fish, on a weekend, ya know."*

Rick looks at you, trying to figure out whether he can trust the gesture of friendship or not.

Rick: *"Maybe. Let me think about it."*

You: *"Definitely."*

You nod toward the door and stand up. When Rick is standing, you reach out to shake hands again.

You: *"Thanks, Rick."*

He shakes your hand and nods silently. As you exit the pub together, you realize that you parked in different directions. You lift one hand and nod to signal a silent wave goodbye and head for your car. After just a few steps you hear Rick's voice and turn to look at him.

Rick: *"Hey, Johnson. Maybe I can talk to Frank. But until I do, keep your head low, OK? I don't wanna have any trouble, ya know what I mean?"*

You nod with understanding and smile.

You: *"I understand."*

Fade to black . . . .

Air Travel Delay

THE PLANE WAS AN HOUR AND A HALF LATE ARRIVING AT THE TERMINAL.
Having finally boarded, you've been sitting on the runway waiting for take off,
for almost forty-five minutes. With a good tail wind this flight takes almost
four hours. And now they've just announced another delay. Ugh! You're tired
from a long week on the road and just want to get home and take your shoes
off. A chorus of sighs and groans from the other passengers accompanies
their adjustment from take-off mode back to wait mode.

You're sitting next to a pleasant enough looking middle-aged woman who,
upon hearing the updated delay announcement, begins to shift around in her
seat. You briefly glance at each other with a look that says, "Oh well, what can
you do?"

Realizing that you're going to be travel partners for some undetermined number of hours, she introduces herself while shuffling through her carry-on bag.

Sharon: *"Hi. I'm Sharon. Looks like we're going to be putting in some time
together. Here, I brought some snacks. Want one?"*

She pulls out a plastic resealable bag with an assortment of delicious-looking
home-baked goodies and holds it open right in front of you. Peering down
into the bag, the smell immediately melts your frustration about the delay
and envelopes you with a warm feeling. Your face relaxes. You look up at her
with a smile, then back into the bag. Reaching in gently, you select an incredibly wholesome looking muffin-like thing.

You: *"Oh, thank you. They look delicious. Did you make them?"*

Sharon: *"Some. Not all of them. They're left over from a conference I was at
yesterday. But still pretty good."*

You: *"Oh, thank you so much. I'm not a big fan of airplane cuisine."*

Sharon: *"Me neither. So I thought I'd better bring a few along for the ride today.
There were so many left over, and sometimes these delays ... well, you know."*

You take a bite and, savoring the wonderful combination of nostalgic flavors and whole grain heft, comment to her.

You: *"Mmm. This is really good."*

[What is that flavor?]

In a voice somewhat muffled by an embarrassingly large mouthful, you continue.

You: *"Mmm. Excoose me. What confoorence were you at?"*

Sharon: *"Oh, no problem. They're a little dry, and kind of hard to eat without making a mess. Well, our church had its annual leadership gathering. We all get together once a year and report on how things are going in our regions. We try to figure out how we can support each other in our mission to reach more people in our areas. That sort of thing."*

You: *"Mmm. Sounds ... good. Do you work for the church?"*

Sharon: *"Oh, heavens no. I've been working for the Stanyon County courthouse for twenty-six years—your basic mid-level bureaucrat. But I've been at the same church even longer. And at this point, I'm the one who knows the most about how the national organization works, so they've been sending me to the conference for the last ten years or so. How about you?"*

You: *"Oh, I'm a traveling sales rep for a pharmaceutical company. I'm on my way home from a week-long training on a new line of medicines that we'll be promoting soon. I can't wait to get home. It's been a long week."*

As you chat about your jobs, families, and current involvements, you learn that she has been married for thirty-three years to a husband who has been in law enforcement for twenty-eight years and is looking forward to retirement. She has four grown children and eleven grandchildren, all living in the same well-groomed, middle-class suburban neighborhood where they enjoy holidays and home-team sports together. She's been very involved, through her church, in various community charity organizations, and is proudly patriotic (which you might have guessed by the flag pin on her lapel and the flag patch on her carry-on bag).

[What an incredible sense of stability, order, and belonging she must have.

Makes my scattered, hectic lifestyle—two kids from two marriages, one still at home, always feeling "on the edge" financially—look pretty pathetic.]

You notice as you chat, that while she is efficiently nibbling away at her whole-grain scone (or whatever it is), she is also meticulously capturing and herding any stray crumbs into a neat little pile on a cloth napkin spread evenly across her lap.

[Very conscientious. A little compulsive maybe, but … effective. Twenty-six years at the same county job? Probably really good with details, rules, and hierarchy. Married for thirty-three years to a cop? Sounds like a real steady person, a real straight arrow. God, I wish I had *my* life under control like that. And she's so friendly, polite, thoughtful, unpretentious. A good person.]

You take another bite. Chewing this time, before speaking.

You: *"Mmm. This is great. Thank you so much."*

As you speak, she reaches into her bag and pulls out another cloth napkin and hands it to you. Noting that you are making a bit of a mess, you brush a few crumbs off your legs onto the floor before taking the napkin and spreading it over your knees.

You: *"Oops. Thanks."*

Sharon: *"No problem."*

Trying to make conversation, you unawarely begin venting your disappointment about the delay.

You: *"Boy, with the price of tickets these days, you'd think they could at least get us where we're going on time."*

Sharon: *"Yes, no kidding. I think my ticket this year was more than double what I paid last year."*

You: *"The price of fuel, I suppose. It seems to be a big factor these days."*

Sharon: *"I suppose."*

Continuing your unconscious complaining, you put forth a point of view that, upon reflection, you realize may, or may not, be shared by everyone.

You: *"It seems like the prices of almost everything have gone up lately. I wonder what will happen to air travel as the oil reserves decline. And can you believe the price of gas at the pump these days?"*

Sharon: *"Oh, I don't know. I've heard that there's plenty of oil to last for hundreds of years yet. And I'm sure they'll figure out something by then."*

[Oops. Go slowly. Stay aware. Don't fall into the divide. Listen. Hear her out.]

You: *"Oh, really? Hmm. That's interesting."*

Sharon: *"Yes. Our pastor did a weeknight series on that a few months ago. He told us that if the darned liberal environmentalists would just stop tying things up with unnecessary regulations and let us drill where the oil is, that we'd have more than enough. Instead, they've got us paying all of our money to foreign terrorists."*

[Darned liberals? Unnecessary regulations? Foreign terrorists? Be careful. Go slowly. Don't offend her. Think. OK. Seems like maybe she's viewing the world from an "Order and Authority" perspective. If so, any signs of disrespect or challenge will only make *me* seem like the enemy—a terrorist sympathizer. Don't say anything crass about her pastor or his sources of information. She probably takes great comfort in deferring to his authority and a clear set of rules to follow in life. Her charity work implies, though, that she really wants to do the "right" thing, and probably *does* feel some moral obligation to society. She seems to be a part of that strong middle-class that simply accepts their place in the system, goes along with the capitalist-driven cultural "marching orders," and gets the job done. It's been good for millions of people, rising standards of living and all. But it's also been at the expense of many poor people in other countries and the environment. It might be that her willingness to defer her own thinking to the opinions of authority is based on an underlying insecurity, perhaps stemming from a harsh upbringing where real scarcity, economic instability, and unreachable perfectionist performance standards drove her to welcome a simplified set of guidelines in return for a promise of something solid to hang onto.]

You: *"Yes, it's so hard to know for sure. I mean, I don't really know, but I've heard some people say that there's not as much oil left as we once thought. And that some of the remaining oil is much harder to get out of the ground."*

Sharon: *"Oh, I don't worry about that sort of thing."*

Sharon goes on to recite a predictably scripted, AM radio sound-bite version of the energy crisis which includes all of the commonly espoused divisive labeling, finger-pointing, scapegoating, and mean-spirited nationalism that seems so contrary to her otherwise pleasant and sociable demeanor.

[Hmm. Seems like a media-induced crust on her underlying sweetness. Really *wants* to please others and is easily swayed in her attempts to "keep the peace." Her worldview probably squelches anything that challenges traditional values and the established chain-of-command. No tolerance for anything that might disrupt order. "Locking horns" will probably only cause the worst aspects of this worldview to become more rigid and intolerant—nationalism and oversimplified black-and-white perceptions of reality. Be respectful and pleasant. Search for common concerns. Maybe just listen for a while and let her unravel her position.]

As you continue to elicit Sharon's opinions about the current state of the world, you notice that whenever you indicate the possibility that change might be upon us, as a civilization, it seems to activate her whole constellation of defensive maneuvers and intensifies the rigidity of her position. This is a good indication that it is best to stay away from talking about peak oil collapse scenarios and steer, instead, toward issues more likely to suit her character structure.

[Maybe "efficiency" in fuel standards might appeal to her conscientiousness. So might re-examining her statement about "unnecessary regulations." If only she could see, as a "steward of God's creation" and an elder for future generations, that "doing the right thing" might include taking a stand against corruption and greed, by employing environmental legislation for the protection of our inheritance. She surely understands and supports the notion that everyone must play by the rules.]

It seems a little abrupt, perhaps, but you decide to risk steering the conversation in the direction of efficiency standards to see if you can find something in common.

You: *"Well, I have to say, I was very impressed with the Evangelical Climate Initiative's 'What would Jesus Drive' campaign. I think that however much oil* *is left, being efficient and not wasteful is a good idea. I like the idea of conserving precious resources and using them wisely rather than wasting them unnecessarily. I also like the idea of recycling, when possible."*

Pleased to not be falling into a divide with you, she responds eagerly with validation of common ground.

Sharon: *"Oh, yes. We recycle a lot. Two of my kids organized the community recycling campaign in our town when they were in college. It's a regular business now. Not for them, of course. And actually, my husband has been leading the charge at the police station to increase the fuel efficiency of the law enforcement fleet. It looks like it's going to go through. The county fleet where I work is also moving in that direction. Yes. We believe in conserving and reusing as much as possible."*

[Phew! All right. That worked. We believe? There's that blind loyalty thing again. Submerging individual identity for the approval and acceptance of others? Is *that* what's going on? What's with that? Where is her "I"? Where does *she* stand? She seems plenty intelligent, just too willing to please. She doesn't want to upset things. Likes her underling position in the hierarchy? Maybe feels "safe" there. I wonder what will happen if I encourage her to express a little more autonomy, a little more individual identity? Start by owning how difficult it can be.]

You: *"Wow. That's impressive. You've done a lot for the good of the environment and future generations. I know for me, sometimes it's hard to know where I stand on some of these issues. I mean I hear one thing here and another thing there. And they all seem to make some sense. Sometimes I just don't know what to believe."*

Sharon: *"Yes, I understand. It gets a little confusing for any of us when we forget what God expects of us."*

[Careful. Think. It's asking a lot of her to question the validity of assumptions that have been handed down by esteemed authority figures, religious institutions, and corporate-sponsored media.]

You: *"Yes. I think I know what you mean. But you know, sometimes, I still wonder about the role of personal responsibility in all of this. What is our responsibility? When does God intend for us to think for ourselves and make*

230

decisions as responsible adults that may, or may not, go along with what we're being told to believe?"

Sharon: *"Oh, yes. It's not always easy."*

You: *"I mean, I think we still have some responsibility for how things turn out."*

Not wanting to cross swords with you, she defers.

Sharon: *"Well, you're probably right. You seem to know more about it than I do."*

[Damn. Seems like she's just going along with me now, saying what she thinks *I* want to hear in order to avoid conflict or disapproval. Hmmm. I'm talking too much.]

You: *"Oh, not really. But I do worry, sometimes, about where things are headed. About the world we're leaving to our grandchildren. I worry that they might not have as wonderful a life as we've had."*

Sharon: *"Well, that's where faith comes in, I guess. We believe that God has a plan, and that if we all just do our best and work hard and stay on the path, that God will make sure it all works out."*

[Hmm. Seems like any consideration of issues like the unraveling of the global economy or peak oil might be too much for her to face without regressing into a defensive posture—too much anxiety and uncertainty. Still, there has to be a way to recognize personal responsibility rather than laying it at the feet of some external power. Think. She needs *something* to hang on to—something solid. I guess her belief system is one way to avoid feeling insecurity and the guilt of complicity. And really, by all outward appearances, her coping strategy is working a helluva lot better than mine. But still... Hmm.]

You: *"That must be a great comfort to you in uncertain times. For me, some-times when the path forward is not clear and it seems like things are not in my hands, I try to trust that everything will work out if I just put one foot in front of the other and try to do the right thing. Other times, though, I feel like I have more responsibility, like I do have some measure of control, through the choices I make, about how things turn out. Sometimes I wonder if society isn't, at some level, just the sum total of all of our individual choices playing out together at the same time. When I feel this way, I feel like it's really important for each* *individual person to be as informed as possible, and to use their best thinking and most compassionate heart to make those choices that will be the best for the most people. Do you know what I mean?"*

This obviously stimulates some recollections in Sharon's mind that she still has some need to talk about and try to make sense of.

Sharon: *"Oh, yes. I know very well what you mean. When my children were teenagers…"*

She goes on to tell a series of stories about how poor choices led to suffering for some of her children when they were growing up, and how she relied on and instilled a sense of right and wrong in them. It becomes apparent, through her narrative, that she doesn't believe that faith supplants responsibility, or that we are destined by fate or God to suffer any particular future. But she *does* maintain a fairly narrow view that, while helping alleviate anxiety about uncertainty in her life, also leaves her individual thinking susceptible to persuasion by those she considers to be like-minded authorities who offer a simplified sense of structure in an otherwise unstructured existence.

[An accepting and validating response will probably reduce her anxiety about pleasing me and allow her to loosen her grip on her worldview enough to consider the role of personal and collective responsibility in the progress of civilization.]

You: *"Yes. I know what you mean. Helping teenagers make good choices can be challenging. Knowing right from wrong is a big part of becoming a responsible adult and citizen. I believe we're all responsible, within reason, for how well society goes. We're continually having to make decisions, based on our own best assessment of a situation, in the face of ever-changing circumstances. In a way, you could say we're co-creating the future together as we go, with our combined choices and actions."*

[That wasn't too bad. A little abstract.]

Sharon: *"Well, I'd have to say, I've never looked at it exactly that way. But I suppose you're right. We're each faced with a lot of little decisions everyday. And together they add up to our whole society. And while God's plan gives us the overall direction, the details are up to us, I suppose."*

[Yes. Right on! She's using her own intelligence to reconsider reality from a slightly different perspective. This is good.]

Meanwhile, unnoticed by the two of you, a flight attendant has been working her way up the aisle and is suddenly upon you. She leans over with a smile and says to you both, "Please put your carry-on bags away and put your seat belts back on. We're getting ready for takeoff."

Fade to black ....

Bibliography

Abrahamson, L., Seligman, M., & Teasdale, J. (1978). Learned helplessness in humans: Critique and reformulation. In *Journal of Abnormal Psychology*, 87, 49–74.

Adler, A. (1938). *Social Interest: A Challenge to Mankind* (J. Linton & R. Vaughan, Trans.). Faber and Faber Ltd.

Adler, A. (1956). H.L. Ansbacher & R.R. Ansbacher (Eds.). *The Individual Psychology of Alfred Adler*. Harper Torchbooks.

Allport, G. (1955). *Becoming*. Yale University Press.

Atlee, T. & Zubizarreta, R. (2003). *The Tao of Democracy: Using Co-Intelligence to Create a World that Works for All*. The Writers Collective.

Bakan, J. (2005). *The Corporation: The Pathological Pursuit of Profit and Power*. Free Press.

Bateson, G. (1972). *Steps to an Ecology of Mind*. University of Chicago Press.

Beck, A., Freeman, A. and Associates. (1990). *Cognitive Therapy of Personality Disorders*. The Guilford Press.

Beck, D. & Cowan, C. (1996). *Spiral Dynamics: Mastering Values, Leadership, and Change*. Blackwell Publishing.

Becker, E. (1973). *Denial of Death*. Free Press.

Bowlby, J. (1969). *Attachment and Loss* (2 Vols.). Basic Books.

Brown, L.R. (2006). *Plan B 2.0: Rescuing a Planet Under Stress and a Civilization in Trouble*. New York: W.W. Norton.

Brown, L. (2001). *Eco-economy: Building an Economy for the Earth*. New York: W.W. Norton.

Buber, M. (1970). *I and Thou*. Charles Scribner.

Bugental, J. (1965). *The Search for Authenticity*. Rinehart & Winston.

Bugental, J. (1967). Someone needs to worry: The existential anxiety of responsibility and decision. In *Journal of Contemporary Psychotherapy*, 2, 41–53.

Capra, F. (2002). *The Hidden Connections*. Anchor Books.

Camus, A. (1972). *A Happy Death*. Alfred A. Knopf.

Carson, R.L. (1962). *Silent Spring*. Houghton Mifflin.

Chomsky, N. (1989). *Necessary Illusions: Thought Control in Democratic Societies*. South End Press.

Chomsky, N. (1992). *Manufacturing Consent: Noam Chomsky and the Media*, documentary. Zeitgeist Films.

Chomsky, N. (1999). *Profit Over People: Neoliberalism and Global Order*, Seven Stories Press.

Combs, A. (2002). *The Radiance of Being: Understanding the Grand Integral Vision; Living the Integral Life* (2nd ed.). Paragon House.

Cook-Greuter, S. (1994). *Transcendence and Mature Thought in Adulthood*. Rowman & Littlefield Publishers.

Csikszentmihalyi, M. (1994). *The Evolving Self*. Harper Perennial.

Csikszentmihalyi, M. (1998). *Finding Flow: The Psychology of Engagement with Everyday Life*. Basic Books.

Daly, H.E. (1990). *Toward some operational principles of sustainable development*, Ecological Economics, Elsevier, 2(1), 1–6, April.

De Graaf, J., Wann, D., & Naylor, T.H. (2005). *Affluenza: The All-Consuming Epidemic*. Berrett-Koehler Publishers.

Diamond, J. (2005). *Collapse: How Societies Choose to Fail or Succeed*. Viking Press.

Dowd, M. (2008). *Thank God for Evolution*. Viking Press.

DSM-IV-TR. (2000). *Diagnostic and Statistical Manual of Mental Disorders* (4th ed., text revision). American Psychiatric Association.

Durning, A. (1992). *How Much Is Enough?: The Consumer Society and the Future of the Earth.* W.W. Norton.

Ecosystems and Human Health. (2007). *Ecosystems and Human Health: Some Findings from the Millennium Ecosystem Assessment: 2-page Summary of Health Synthesis.* Retrieved January 2007: http://www.maweb.org/en/index.aspx.

Ehrlich, P. & Ehrlich, A. (2004). *One with Nineveh: Politics, Consumption, and the Human Future.* Washington, D.C.: Island Press.

EPA (2007). United States Environmental Protection Agency, Environmental Education Division (EED), Office of Children's Health Protection and Environmental Education. Retrieved January 2007: http://www.epa.gov/enviroed.

Erikson, E. (1963). *Childhood and Society* (2nd ed.). W.W. Norton.

Festinger, L. (1957). *A Theory of Cognitive Dissonance.* Row, Peterson.

Frankl, V. (1963). *Man's Search for Meaning.* Beacon Press.

Frankl, V. (1969). *The Will to Meaning.* New American Library.

Freud, A. (1946). *The Ego and the Mechanisms of Defense.* International University Press.

Freud, S. (1957). *Some Character Types Met with in Psychoanalytic Work* (standard ed., Vol. XIV). Hogarth Press.

Freud, S. (1961). *The Psychopathology of Everyday Life.* (standard ed., Vol. VI). Hogarth Press.

Friedman, T. (2006). *The World Is Flat: A Brief History of the Twenty-First Century.* Farrar, Straus and Giroux Pub.

Fromm, E. (1941). *Escape from Freedom.* Holt, Rinehart & Winston).

Gardener, G. & Assadourian, E. (2004). Rethinking the good life. In *State of the World 2004* by The Worldwatch Institute. W.W. Norton.

Gebser, J. (1985). *The Ever-Present Origin* (N. Barstad & A. Mickunas, Trans.). Ohio University Press.

Gerzon, M. (1997). *A House Divided: Six Belief Systems Struggling for America's Soul.* Tarcher Press.

Gilligan, C., Ward, J., Taylor, J. M., & Bardige, B. (Eds.). (1988). *Mapping the Moral Domain: A Contribution of Women's Thinking to Psychological Theory and Education.* Harvard University Press.

Graves, C.W. (1970). *Levels of existence: An open system theory of values.* In *Journal of Humanistic Psychology,* November 1970.

Graves, C.W. (1974). Human nature prepares for a momentous leap. In *The Futurist,* April 1974.

Greenwald, H. (1973). *Decision Therapy.* Peter Wyden.

Hall, C. & Lindzey, G. (1978). *Theories of Personality* (3rd ed.). John Wiley & Sons.

Hardin, G. (1968). Tragedy of the commons. In *Science,* 162, 1243–48.

Hartmann, T. (2006). *Screwed: The Undeclared War Against the Middle Class and What We Can Do About It.* Berrett-Koehler Publishers.

Heinberg, R. (2003). *The Party's Over: Oil, War and the Fate of Industrial Societies.* New Society Publishers.

Heinberg, R. (2004). *PowerDown: Options and Actions for a Post-Carbon World.* New Society Publishers.

Heinberg, R. (2007). *Peak Everything: Waking Up to the Century of Declines.* New Society Publishers.

Hiroto, D. (1974). Locus of control and learned helplessness. In *Journal of Experimental Psychology,* 102, 187–93.

Horney, K. (1950). *Neurosis and Human Growth.* W.W. Norton.

Johnson, A. (2006). *Privilege, Power and Difference* (2nd ed.). McGraw Hill.

Jung, C. (1933). *Modern Man in Search of a Soul.* Hartcourt.

Kanner, A.D., Roszak, T., & Gomes, M.E. (1995). *Ecopsychology: Restoring the Earth, Healing the Mind.* Sierra Club Books.

Kegan, R. (1982). *The Evolving Self.* Harvard University Press.

Kernberg, O. (1993). *Severe Personality Disorders: Psychotherapeutic Strategies.* Yale University Press.

Kierkegaard, J., in Becker, E. (1973). *The Denial of Death.* Free Press.

Kierkegaard, J. (1954). *Fear and Trembling / The Sickness unto Death* (W. Lowrie, Trans.). Doubleday, Anchor.

Kierkegaard, S. (1944). *Either/Or* (D. Swanson, Trans.). Princeton University Press.

Kohlberg, L. & Lickona, T. (Eds.). (1976). Moral stages and moralization: The cognitive-developmental approach. In *Moral Development and Behavior: Theory, Research and Social Issues.* Rinehart and Winston.

Kohlberg, L. (1981). *Essays on Moral Development,* Vol. I: The Philosophy of Moral Development. Harper & Row.

Korten, D. (2000). *The Post-Corporate World: Life After Capitalism.* Berrett-Koehler Publishers.

Korten, D. (2002). *When Corporations Rule the World.* Berrett-Koehler Publishers.

Korten, D. (2006). *The Great Turning: From Empire to Earth Community.* Berrett-Koehler Publishers.

Kubler-Ross, E. (1969). *On Death & Dying.* Simon & Schuster.

Kuhn, T. (1962). *The Structure of Scientific Revolutions.* University of Chicago Press.

Kunstler, J.H. (2006). *The Long Emergency: Surviving the Converging Catastrophes of the Twenty-first Century.* Grove Press.

Kurtz, R. (1990). *Body-Centered Psychotherapy: The Hakomi Method,* (LifeRhythm).

Lakoff, G. (2004). *Don't Think of an Elephant: Know Your Values and Frame the Debate—The Essential Guide for Progressives.* Chelsea Green.

Langs, R. (1982). *Psychotherapy: A Basic Text.* Jason Aronson, Inc.

Langs, R. (1973). *The Techniques of Psychoanalytic Psychotherapy* (Vols. I–II). Jason Aronson, Inc.

Lappe, F.M. (1971). *Diet for a Small Planet.* Ballantine.

Loevinger, J. (1970). *Measuring Ego Development.* Jossey-Bass.

Loevinger, J. (1976). *Ego Development.* Jossey-Bass.

Loevinger, J. (1987). *Paradigms of Personality.* Freeman.

Logan, R. (2005). *PROUT: A New Paradigm of Development.* Ananda Seva Pub.

Lorey, D. (Ed.). (2003). *Global Environmental Challenges of the Twenty-first Century: Resources, Consumption, and Sustainable Solutions.* Wilmington, Delaware: Scholarly Resources.

Macy, J. & Brown, M.Y. (1998). *Coming Back To Life: Practices to Reconnect Our Lives, Our World.* New Society Publishers.

Magnuson, J. (2007). *Mindful Economics.* Seven Stories Press.

Mander, J. (1978). *Four Arguments for the Elimination of Television.* Harper Perennial.

Mander, J. (1992). *In the Absence of the Sacred: The Failure of Technology and the Survival of the Indian Nations.* Sierra Club Books.

Maslow, A. (1962). *Toward a Psychology of Being.* Van Nostrand.

Maslow, A. (1971). *The Further Reaches of Human Nature.* Viking.

Masterson, J. (1985). *The Real Self.* Brunner/Mazel, Inc.

Masterson, J. (1993). *The Emerging Self.* Brunner/Mazel, Inc.

May, R., Angel, E., & Ellensberger, H. (1958). *Existence.* Basic Books.

May, R. (1977). *The Meaning of Anxiety.* W.W. Norton.

McKibben, B. (2007). *Deep Economy: The Wealth of Communities and the Durable Future.* Times Books.

Meadows, D., Randers, J., & Meadows, D. (2005). *Limits to Growth: The Thirty Year Update.* Chelsea Green.

Millennium Ecosystem Assessment (2005). *Ecosystems and Human Well-being: Synthesis.* Washington, D.C.: Island Press.

Millon, T., Millon, C., Davis, R., & Grossman, S. (1997). *MCMI–III: Millon Clinical Multiaxial Inventory-III* (2nd ed.). National Computer Systems, Inc.

NIEHS (2007a). National Institute of Environmental Health Sciences, Division of Extramural Research and Training, Small Business Innovative Research—Topics of Special Interest, *Educational Material Program.* Retrieved February 2007: http://www.niehs.nih.gov/dert/programs/sbir/educate.htm.

NIEHS (2007b). National Institute of Environmental Health Sciences, Division of Extramural Research and Training, Translational Research, Environmental Health Sciences K–12 Education Program. Retrieved February 2007: http://www.niehs.nih.gov/translat/k12/k12educa.htm.

OECD, *Towards Sustainable Consumption: An Economic Conceptual Framework.* Paris: Environment Directorate, June 2002, p. 29. Organisation for Economic Co-operation and Development.

Oldham, J. & Morris, L. (1995). *The New Personality Self-Portrait: Why You Think, Work, Love and Act the Way You Do.* Bantam.

Perls, F. (1971). *Gestalt Therapy Verbatim.* Bantam.

Pimm, S. (2001). *The World According to Pimm: A Scientist Audits the Earth.* New York: McGraw-Hill.

Prescott-Allen, R. (2001). *The Well-being of Nations: A Country-by-Country Index of Quality of Life and the Environment.* Washington: Island Press.

Reich, W. & Carfagno, V. (1980). *Character Analysis.* Farrar, Straus and Giroux.

Roberts, P. (2005). *The End of Oil: On the Edge of a Perilous New World.* Mariner Books.

Rogers, C. (1951). *Client-Centered Therapy.* Houghton Mifflin Co.

Rogers, C. (1961). *On Becoming a Person.* Houghton Mifflin Co.

Rosenberg, H. (1963). The fear of death as an indispensable factor in psychotherapy. In *American Journal of Psychotherapy,* 17, 619–630.

Rosenberg, M. (2003). *Nonviolent Communication: A Language of Compassion.* Puddledancer Press.

Ryckman, R. & Sherman, M. (1971). Relationship between self-esteem and internal locus of control. In *Psychological Report,* 32, 1106.

Sartre, J. (1965). *The Transcendence of the Ego: An Existentialist Theory of Consciousness.* Noonday Press.

Schumacher, E.F. (1973). *Small is Beautiful: Economics As If People Mattered.* Harper.

Seligman, M. & Maier, S. (1967). Failure to escape traumatic shock. In *Journal of Experimental Psychology,* 74, 1–9.

Seligman, M. (1975). *Helplessness: On Depression, Development, and Death.* W.H. Freeman.

Seligman, M. (1990). *Learned Optimism.* Free Press.

Shapiro, D. (1965). *Neurotic Styles.* Basic Books.

Shapiro, D. (1981). *Autonomy and Rigid Character.* Basic Books.

Shapiro, D. (1989). *Psychotherapy of Neurotic Character.* Basic Books.

Simmons, M. (2005). *Twilight in the Desert: The Coming Saudi Oil Shock and the World Economy.* Wiley Press.

Sleeth, J.M. (2006). *Serve God Save the Planet.* Chelsea Green.

Smil, V. (2003). *Energy at the Crossroads: Global Perspectives and Uncertainties.* Cambridge, Massachusetts: MIT Press.

Smith, A. (1776). *An Inquiry Into the Nature and Causes of the Wealth of Nations.* University of Chicago Press.

Tillich, P. (1952). *The Courage to Be.* Yale University Press.

Tolle, E. (2008). *A New Earth: Awakening To Your Life's Purpose.* Penguin.

Union of Concerned Scientists. (1992). *World Scientists Warning to Humanity,* (Cambridge, Massachusetts) www.ucsusa.org.

United Nations. (2002). *Report of the World Summit on Sustainable Development*, A/CONF.199/20, New York.

United Nations. (1998). United Nations Development Program, *Human Development Report 1998*. Oxford University Press.

USDHHS. (2000). U.S. Department of Health and Human Services, *Healthy People 2010: Understanding and Improving Health* (2nd ed., 2 Vols.). (2000). Washington, D.C., U.S. Government Printing Office.

Wackernagel, M. et al. (2002). *Tracking the Ecological Overshoot of the Human Economy*, Proceedings of the Academy of Science 99, 14, 9266–9271.

Watson, R.T. et al. (2001). *Climate Change 2001: Synthesis Report, Inter-governmental Panel on Climate Change*. Geneva, Switzerland: IPCC, 2001.

Wilber, K. (1996). *A Brief History of Everything*. Shambhala Press.

World Bank. (2001a). *Making Sustainable Commitments: An Environmental Strategy*, Washington, D.C., April 2001.

World Bank (2001b). *World Development Indicators—2001*. Washington, D.C.: World Bank, 2001.

Worldwatch Institute. (1984–2005). *State of the World*. W.W. Norton & Co.

Worldwatch Institute. (2004). *State of the World: 2004, Progress Toward a Sustainable Society*. W.W. Norton & Co.

Yalom, I. (1980). *Existential Psychotherapy*. Basic Books.

Zimbardo, P.G. (1969). *Influencing Attitudes and Changing Behavior*. Addison Wesley.

Zimbardo, P.G. (1991). *The Psychology of Attitude Change and Social Influence*. McGraw Hill.